FIELD OF *Memories*

A Tapestry of
HEARTWARMING
SHORT STORIES

D. L. NORRIS

Spring River Press

Field of Memories
A Tapestry of Heartwarming Short Stories
All Rights Reserved.
Copyright © 2026 D. L. Norris
v2.0

The opinions expressed in this manuscript are solely the opinions of the author and do not represent the opinions or thoughts of the publisher. The author has represented and warranted full ownership and/or legal right to publish all the materials in this book.

This book may not be reproduced, transmitted, or stored in whole or in part by any means, including graphic, electronic, or mechanical without the express written consent of the publisher except in the case of brief quotations embodied in critical articles and reviews.

Spring River Press

Paperback ISBN: 979-8-9880798-1-1
Hardback ISBN: 979-8-9880798-0-4

Cover Photo © 2026 www.gettyimages.com. All rights reserved - used with permission.

PRINTED IN THE UNITED STATES OF AMERICA

Dedicated

To my precious mama,
a steadfast supporter, never tiring encourager, and
forever my dearest friend.
Oh, how I miss her.

Table of Contents

From the Author	i
Foreword	iii
The Early Years	
1. A Dream is a Wish Your Heart Makes	2
2. Levi's, Doris Day, and Penny Candy	4
3. Tell Me a Story	6
4. Black Forest Beauty	8
5. Big Jim and the Lost Dime	10
6. The Teacher and the China Doll	12
7. Days of Matthew	14
8. Girls and Curls	16
9. Sweet Rosemary	18
10. Miss Boots	20
11. Color Them Magical	22
12. Dora Jane	24
13. Because of Goldie	26
14. Sweetpea	28
15. Yellow Roses	30
16. Clarence and Lena	32

17. Roosevelt Market	34
18. Saturday Morning Glory	36
19. Sunday Afternoon Drive	38
20. Rose of Remembrance	40
21. A Picnic in the Park	42
22. The Upholstery Bus	44
23. Good as Gold	46
24. The Porch Light	48
25. Roughing It	50

Coming of Age

26. The Day I Became a Woman	53
27. Thirteen Chicks	55
28. Squirrel Blues	57
29. Transformative Years	58
30. The Great Escape	66

Days of Promise

31. Rose-Colored Glasses	69
32. Night Stalker	73
33. Christmas Came Early	76

Life Unfolding

34. Decade of Decadence	79
35. Far East Princess	84

Dawn of a New Day

36. See You Later, Kid	87

37. Never Forget	89
38. Keeper of Memories	92

A Change of Season	**94**
39. Second Chances	95
40. Finishing Well	97
41. Imaginary Horse	99
42. When I Leave	101
43. Bearing One Another's Burdens	104
44. Ageless Beauty	106
45. Touched By an Angel	108
46. A Life Well-Lived	110
47. Thief of Memories	112
48. Thanks for the Memories	115

The Stories They Told	**117**
49. Tenderhearted Charmer	118
50. Faded Dreams	120
51. Sworn to Secrecy	123
52. A Better Tomorrow	126
53. The Red Bean	128
54. The Kitchen Chair	130
55. Mama's Red Boots	132
56. The Old Opera House	134
57. Night Rider	136

Afterword	138

From the Author

For as long as I can remember, my mind has been a gallery of vivid snapshots—remarkable moments, fleeting emotions, and treasured experiences, each carefully stored and lovingly revisited through the years. These long-ago images, meticulously cataloged in the archives of memory, remain as clear today as they were in the days first experienced. Time, it seems, has only served to deepen their color and meaning.

It was my beloved mother, wise with her ninety years of living, who offered the most profound advice: "If you don't write everything down, the stories will be gone when you are." Her words resonated deeply, echoing with the urgency to preserve not just facts, but the essence of a life well-lived—the laughter, lessons, and love. She was right, of course. Stories are the threads that bind generations, and without them, the tapestry of family and identity begins to unravel.

Inspired by her gentle insistence, I embarked on the journey of putting my story to paper. What began as a simple act of remembrance soon became an extraordinary adventure—one that allowed me to relive the days and revisit the cherished happenings that shaped who I am. Each memory, whether joyful or bittersweet, became a steppingstone along the path of self-discovery.

Writing these stories has been more than a creative pursuit; it has been a process of healing and celebration. I have found myself laughing anew at childhood antics, shedding tears for losses that still ache, and marveling at the resilience that carried me through seasons of change. In capturing these moments, I have come to appreciate the quiet strength of my family, the enduring wisdom of my mother, and the simple joys that make life beautiful.

It is my hope that as you read these pages, you will find echoes of your own journey—reminders of the people and places that have shaped you, and encouragement to cherish your memories as the priceless treasures they are. May the stories invite you to reflect, to dream, and to honor the legacy of love that connects us all.

Thank you for joining me on this journey through a field of memories. It is my hope that you will enjoy reading this tapestry of heartwarming short stories as much as I have cherished writing them.

Warmly,
D. L. Norris

Foreword

Relaxing in our comfortable chairs, we enjoyed a second cup of coffee, my sweet mama and me. Then, without much notice, she looked over the rim of her cup and stated with determined purpose, "Let's take a little trip upstairs." Her soft blue eyes twinkled at the thought of a trek to the second floor. I offered to bring a few photographs and select family keepsakes downstairs, hoping to discourage her from a laborious climb to the upper level of our home. But the attempt, albeit honorable on my part, failed to dissuade her this time.

She insisted on making the arduous journey, taking her time with each step, fifteen in all. Finally reaching the upper-story landing, we walked along the hallway, where an impressive display of framed ancestry lined the walls. Unfortunately, most of these behind-the-glass family members passed away long before I was born. She spoke as though she had visited each of them the week before. Suddenly, strangers with stoic faces and vague histories came to life with her many vivid recollections. She spoke tenderly of her beloved grandpa, who had a strict ritual he followed each evening at bedtime. First, he would wind the old clock. Then, he went to bed – even if company was visiting – wearing long underwear, a shirt, and a tie. He grew cotton for many years and sold homegrown vegetables from a horse-drawn cart. A favorite pastime of Grandpa was a hearty, if not sometimes rather heated, discussion of religion with his son-in-law. In later years, he traded his strong opinions for reflective respites on his front porch swing as he watched his grandchildren play underneath the persimmon trees.

An old photograph of her grandma brought another flood of memories. She fondly remembered her as a very compassionate person who always found great satisfaction in doing things for others. She was a midwife and assisted with the delivery of many babies. Wherever there was a sick child, you would find her, comforting and attempting to make them well. Unfortunately, she was all but helpless when it came to helping her own ill child, and at the age of six months, one of her twins passed away suddenly. She desperately grieved the loss of her baby and was often inconsolable. Then, one night, the story is told of her waking to see the baby playing happily on her bed. She watched for quite some time, totally enamored by this child she recognized as her own. No one ever convinced her otherwise that God was keeping her baby safe and had graciously allowed her to see for herself that he was well cared for. Though she would be forever mindful of the death of her sweet baby boy, this heaven-sent experience would reside deep within her very soul and comfort her for the rest of her days. Grandchildren always knew their grandma would have something good to eat at her house, whether it was leftover bacon and eggs in the oven, or her signature white cake topped with applesauce and red, cinnamon-heart candies. She raised turkeys, geese, and chickens and churned her own butter. It goes without saying that holiday dinners were a most joyous occasion. She could not read or write, although this proved to be an insignificant handicap. Grandma owned and operated a market for many years. Due to her inability to read, she devised a rather ingenious system for identifying items and their prices with drawings she created.

We entered one of the guest bedrooms, and I removed several handmade items from an old chest of drawers. Again, a heartwarming story from the past accompanied each treasured keepsake. I watched as she ran her fingers along the delicate edges of a crocheted doily that was 75 years old. Seeing an old, well-worn tablecloth that had once graced the little kitchen table in her and Dad's first apartment brought a tear to her eye. Then there was the blue-and-white tablecloth with a ragged tear in the center. She shook her head while closely examining the unsightly rip in the cloth. "This was *my* mama's favorite tablecloth," she began, still shaking her head as she recalled the infamous moment. "The dog next door was watching as she hung the tablecloth on the clothesline one morning. Without so much as a warning, he ran toward the clothesline and grabbed the tablecloth in his mouth and shook it," she said, looking disgusted. "This hole, mind you, is the handiwork of that silly dog."

She journeyed bygone years with ease, like a familiar well-traveled path, and with a strange clarity that often eluded her when she tried to recall what she did earlier in the day. The places in her mind where she chose to stop and sit for a while became vibrant stories that she articulated like a gifted orator. Suddenly, I saw her as a beautifully written novel, pages worn but rich with prose. I felt so humbled to "read" with her.

At the end of it all, her expression was pure joy. "Well, that was delightful," she said with a smile. "I feel like I've been on a nice trip." Indeed, she had, and I felt privileged to have accompanied her on a breathtaking excursion through a colorful field of memories.

The Early Years

*A childhood so rich,
With memories richer still.*

My childhood years were remarkably unique, wonderfully nurturing, and gloriously fulfilling. I am blessed and recognize the wealth therein. I am humbly grateful to those who were the nurturers—they gave me life and a reason. I am thankful beyond measure for the storytellers—they modeled, by example the ability to dream, imagine, and create.

Butterflies, Unicorns and Nursery Rhymes
Childhood days, such curious times
Butterflies, unicorns, and nursery rhymes
The questions we asked of elders so wise,
The how-come's and wherefores, on answers we relied.
Time travels on, and simple dreams fade.
Sure to remain, are the memories made.
~ D. L. Norris

A Dream is a Wish Your Heart Makes

*A weeklong adventure with Dad
became the catalyst for living my own fairytale.*

With her blue suitcases packed and sitting next to the front door, Mom was ecstatic that the day had finally arrived for the long-anticipated dream trip to Southern California. She and the church choir were traveling on a big tour bus to Anaheim for the invitation-only dedication of Walt Disney's famous theme park. Disneyland, built on 160 acres of former orange groves, featured five theme lands: Main Street USA, Adventureland, Fantasyland, Tomorrowland, and Frontierland. This exciting grand opening was a momentous occasion, attracting nearly 28,000 guests and celebrities such as Art Linkletter, Fess Parker, Buddy Ebsen, and Ronald Reagan, among others. The dedication was also broadcast live to an estimated ninety million viewers, making it one of the largest of its time.

It was July 1955, and I stood solemnly next to my dad in the church's parking lot to bid farewell to Mom and the other jubilant choir members. With that, the double-decker Greyhound Scenicruiser pulled away slowly from the church and made its way down the frontage road. A smile quickly appeared on my face. I'd be staying home with Dad, and everything had the makings of a picnic in my *own* theme park.

Of course, I didn't wear any of the clothes Mom laid out for me; instead, I selected my own for the next few days while she was gone. Nothing matched. Dad didn't even care that I wore my black patent leather Sunday school shoes, lace-trimmed socks, red-flowered shorts, and an orange-striped T-shirt—every day—for a week. Best of all, he didn't mind that I played with Marie, who was four years older than me and several inches taller. Dad and I ate different things, like hot dogs and root beer floats from Fosters Freeze, instead of food cooked in the kitchen. Regular bedtimes were replaced with falling asleep on the sofa while watching Gene Autry, Wyatt Earp, and Death Valley Days with Dad. Needless to say, baths were few and far between. I was living the dream.

As fate would have it, my Disney dream was short-lived. When Mom got home a week later, I was ushered straight to the bathtub. My shorts, T-shirt, underwear, and lace socks went to the laundry room just as fast. The black Sunday school shoes were scuffed beyond repair and thrown away. In no time, my hair was washed, curled, and pulled back with matching barrettes. Clothes were color-coordinated once again. The aroma of fried chicken and biscuits wafted from the kitchen. Mom was back, and with her reappearance came the warm feeling of life as it was supposed to be.

After she had everything in suitable order, Mom surprised me with a little blue record player, an assortment of Disney records, and Mickey Mouse ears. I was in heaven. The sound of Cinderella singing, "A Dream is a Wish Your Heart Makes," was heard throughout the house for the next several weeks.

Levi's, Doris Day, and Penny Candy

Nothing was quite as exciting in my young life as waiting for the candy truck's arrival and entering the magical world of sweet treats.

It was 1956, and the summer of my fifth year. We lived in Vallejo, California, and my mom worked a short distance away at Levi Strauss Company. It was her job to make and sew pockets on the 501 jeans—as well as stitch the red Levi tab to the right back pocket to differentiate their product from competitors. Simply put, I stayed with Aunt Maggie for several hours until my mom arrived to pick me up in the late afternoon.

Mom drove a green 1948 Studebaker Commander with a radio that was always tuned to San Francisco station KSFO. On our way to Aunt Maggie's house in the morning, we'd listen to our favorite songs and join in with Doris Day:

> *When I was just a little girl*
> *I asked my mother, "What will I be?*
> *Will I be pretty? Will I be rich?"*
> *Here's what she said to me.*

Que sera, sera
Whatever will be, will be.
The future's not ours to see.
Que sera, sera
What will be, will be.

Aunt Maggie also had a radio in her living room, so Perry Como, Frank Sinatra, and Pat Boone always crooned in the background. My love for music likely had its roots in the Studebaker and Aunt Maggie's living room.

Each morning, when I arrived, Aunt Maggie would whisper for me to lie on the sofa, listen to the radio, and be very quiet until my cousins, Steve and Sherry, woke up. Softly, I'd hum along with Perry Como's "Catch a Falling Star," Frank Sinatra's "That Old Feeling," and Pat Boone's "Love Letters in the Sand." It wasn't long before the bedroom door opened just a little, and the cousins peeked through the tiny crack. Oh, how I loved them both.

Once they had eaten their breakfast, we'd surround ourselves with a mountain of big red books. Since neither of us were able to read yet, we'd spend countless hours just looking at all the pictures in The American People's Encyclopedia set, twenty delightful volumes in all.

The highlight of the day was when Aunt Maggie gave each of us a small glass jar with a few pennies in it for candy. The old red and white Hammond's Express candy truck made its way throughout the neighborhood daily—and we knew this because we were watching intently for its arrival. The minute the truck came into view, we bolted off the front porch and stood excitedly at the curb's edge—barefoot and all. We'd greet the candy man and then step inside the back of the truck to choose our sweet treats: Sugar Babies, Bit O' Honey, and Smarties were the usual selections, but we still took our time perusing the many mouth-watering possibilities displayed in the rows of candy jars. It was truly a magical place!

At the late afternoon, Mom arrived to pick me up in the Studebaker. On the way home, we talked about the day, listened to our favorite radio station, sang along with Doris Day, and shared a piece of Beeman's chewing gum. Life was good.

Tell Me a Story

*She hung on every word, smiling,
while whisked to a faraway, magical land.*

My mother loved to read, and I was often the happy recipient of her uncanny ability to bring a story to life. I would sit comfortably on her lap or plopped cross-legged on the floor in front of her chair to be whisked to a faraway, magical land.

The Velveteen Rabbit. I was utterly engrossed in every word of Margery Williams' delightful tale, allowing my young mind to imagine the well-worn little rabbit snuggling with the boy or his deep conversations with the Skin Horse. "Real isn't how you are made," said the Skin Horse. "It's a thing that happens to you. When a child loves you for a long, long time, not just to play with, but REALLY loves you, then you become Real." Of course, this one quote opened up an entire world of fantasy for me. If this were true, then my whole stuffed animal and doll collections would also have the potential to become real. It was a life-changing concept for an imaginative seven-year-old.

And then there was *The Ugly Duckling* by Hans Christian Andersen. Tears would well up in my eyes when my mother read about the little duckling being ostracized by his siblings and other farm animals simply because he was different. The redeeming finale of *The Ugly Duckling,* transformed into a beautiful swan, never failed to bring a round of cheers.

Of course, *Cinderella* was my hero, both when she was a mistreated young stepsister and later when she became a lovely princess. I knew that all things were possible when one truly believed, because Cinderella said so. Besides, she had Gus the mouse to substantiate her claims.

There was *Charlotte's Web* by E.B. White, *The Secret Garden* by Frances Hodgson Burnett, and a score of other classics never to be forgotten and first introduced to me by my mother.

My precious mama left with the angels on a brisk October day, and life just hasn't been quite the same without her. That said, what an incredible legacy she imparted. A couple of years before she died, her eyesight had diminished to such a degree that she was unable to see the print in her treasured books. It was then that I had the absolute joy of reading to *her.* Just like me so many years before, she hung on every word, smiling while being whisked to a faraway, magical land.

Black Forest Beauty

"Don't force the cuckoo to sing before its time."

The German-made cuckoo clock hung proudly in our living room for as long as I can remember. Whenever we moved to a new house, the hand-carved Black Forest beauty was the first thing to be placed on the wall. I really don't recall a time when I didn't hear the subtle tick-tock in the background, and the "cuckoo" of the little hand-painted bird that popped out on the hour—always accompanied by a soothing, melodic tune. Seventy years later, the bird is still at it, and the clock keeps perfect time.

My dad bought the exquisite cuckoo clock from a shopkeeper in Vallejo, California, in 1955, as an anniversary gift for my mother. He was pleased to tell her, while he gently hung the clock on our living room wall, that she now possessed a piece of Bavaria. Well, anyway, it *was* beautiful, with its delicately sculpted leaves and birds. I was fascinated with the heavy, black weights that were shaped like pinecones.

As a curious five-year-old, I vividly recall several instructions from my dad regarding cuckoo clock protocol. An oft-heard reprimand was a simple, yet direct, "Debbie, don't force the cuckoo to sing before its time." Need I say that an hour is an eternity for a five-year-old?

Before going to bed each night, Dad wound the clock and double-checked the front door lock, in that order. Years later, when I lived on my own, there were many sleepless nights as I adjusted to the absence of the calming tick-tock.

Dad was ninety-two when he finally relinquished his cherished cuckoo clock into my care. With gentle resignation in his voice, he said, "It's time for the old clock to have a new home." Then, with a twinkle in his eye and a faint smile, he reminded, "Don't force the cuckoo to sing before its time." I assured him that the treasured piece would receive the best of care—and a place of honor in *my* home. I'm still keeping that promise.

Big Jim and the Lost Dime

Making amends and finding forgiveness along the way.

One of the very first grace-filled moments that I can recall took place when I was about seven years old. It was a life-changing experience, to say the least.

Big Jim was a soft-spoken man and the owner of a small gas station in Vallejo, California, that I passed by each day on my way to and from the neighborhood elementary school. On one especially warm afternoon, as I was walking home, I couldn't help but notice the big red soda machine sitting just inside the station. I had to get a better look at the cold bottles of Coca-Cola, even though I knew full well that I didn't have a dime to my name that day. Big Jim saw me. "Hey, Blondie, what can I do for you today?" Big Jim's question caught me off guard. But I was even more surprised at the words that came out of *my* mouth. "I-I think I lost my dime in your machine," I stuttered, not making eye contact. Big Jim intently checked the machine for the "lost" dime. Without so much as a word, he reached into his shirt pocket for a dime, dropped it into the machine, and then handed me the frosty bottle of Coca-Cola that I so longed for, at least once upon a time.

My heart pounded like a sledgehammer, and my cheeks burned with shame. I walked home much faster that day, a whole bottle of Coca-Cola in tow. I was so upset by the time I reached our house that I swung open the front door and ran inside. "Mom, I did a terrible thing!" I tearfully confessed, nearly hysterical by now. After revealing the entire story, I took a deep breath and lowered my head. What a premium opportunity for a parental reprimand! But I suspect that Mom could see I didn't need to be convinced of my crime. Instead of scolding me, she comforted me and said that she was proud of my honest confession. Then, in a soft yet firm tone, she informed me that I would be returning to the gas station, along with a bottle of Coca-Cola and an apology.

I died a thousand deaths! But before I could protest, we were on our way back to the station. I can see that little gas station as clearly in my mind today as I did that afternoon so many years ago. Big Jim stood near the soda machine, as if he had been anticipating my return. The sight of my friend brought a flood of new tears. Approaching him with my head down, I struggled to express my remorse. "I-I'm so sorry, Jim," I sobbed, handing him the bottle of Coca-Cola. I was surprised again, this time to feel the gentle touch of a hand on my shoulder and the comforting words, "I'm proud of you, Blondie, for coming back and doing the right thing."

Those who extend the hand of grace and forgiveness often do much more than they realize. I learned so much that afternoon. I received a blessing from my mother, whose grace was not cheap. She loved me and forgave me. However, in her wisdom, she did not spare me the discomfort of owning up to my wrongdoing. And I received another blessing from my friend, Big Jim. He forgave me and affirmed me. But he also demonstrated, through his actions, something I would not soon forget. He purchased the bottle of Coca-Cola with his own dime, even though he knew I was guilty of lying. Then, he waited patiently for my return.

The Teacher and the China Doll

At the time, Mrs. Betts didn't realize the life-long impact of her act of kindness. Years later, her sacrifice still resonates.

She was so beautiful, and I could hardly wait until school on Monday to share her with my first-grade classmates. Mom and Dad had gone to San Francisco with their good friends to have dinner at Fisherman's Wharf. After dinner, they strolled around Chinatown, and Mom spotted the porcelain doll in the window of a shop. She and Dad bought the beautiful China doll and gave her to me the following morning. I was so excited that all I could think of was Monday and my turn at Show and Tell.

When Mrs. Betts finally motioned for me to come forward with my doll, in my eagerness, and as fate would have it, I accidentally dropped her on the hardwood floor. To my utter horror, the porcelain head shattered into more pieces than I could count. I was heartsick and immediately felt the hot tears form in my eyes. Mrs. Betts rushed to pick up all the tiny bits, gave me a comforting hug, and then took the damaged doll back to her desk.

Throughout the day, my compassionate first-grade teacher not only tended to her lively and sometimes unruly students, but also painstakingly glued each of the porcelain headpieces in place—a labor of love.

I still have the China doll, and she is over sixty-five years now. Unbelievably, there are little more than hairline imperfections on her face. I will never forget my teacher, Mrs. Betts, and her unforgettable act of kindness.

Days of Matthew

I was too young to understand the meaning of the word racism, but not too young to discover the ways in which it would change my world.

Our eyes met from across the craft table, and it was love at first sight. His dark brown eyes and my light blues. He smiled, and my heart skipped a beat. And then he asked the question that would change my world forever, "Do you want to use my scissors?"

My second-grade days were brighter because of Matthew Johnson. He was always smiling, especially when he saw *me*. My teacher was quick to tell me that it would probably be best if I didn't spend so much time with Matthew during recess and on the playground. "You should stay with your own kind." My *own kind*? I clearly didn't understand what Mrs. Miller was implying. No doubt, Matthew's skin was darker than mine, but it didn't matter to me. He was my very best friend, and we were inseparable.

The long-awaited day finally arrived for Matthew to come over to my house after school. We walked hand in hand to the front door, where Mom greeted us with a smile, chocolate chip cookies, and cold milk. I knew she would like my friend Matthew, and, as I had presumed, she most certainly did. Mom had a way of making young people feel comfortable and welcome. Matthew chatted with her in his own amicable way.

Suddenly, our happy conversation was interrupted by loud pounding on the front door. An angry man stood on the porch, screaming, "That n----r doesn't belong in this neighborhood!" The commotion petrified Matthew, and he ran out the door, past the red-faced man, and down the street. I started to cry. This would be my first experience with racism and hatred, though certainly not my last.

Sadly, my world changed that day. My innocence and my belief that everyone was the same were forever tarnished. The ugly truth had been revealed at that moment, and I began to see that not everyone viewed things the way *I* did.

Matthew's happy smile faded, and Mrs. Miller moved *me* to another part of the classroom where I was seated with my own kind. Second-grade days weren't so bright anymore.

Childhood Innocence
Childhood innocence, so pure and unstained
A youthful view of life, I wish could remain.
Such joy in the moment, sweet smiles of regard
Unbiased, unfettered, hearts without guard.
Free to love, equally, the same.
Childhood innocence, so pure and unstained.
~ D. L. Norris

Girls and Curls

Who knew that a simple home perm had the power to establish trends and change lives.

My first *Toni* home permanent took place in the summer of 1957, coinciding with a photo session that was scheduled a few days after the infamous hair transformation. I've often thought that Mom's timing was short-sighted, and the photos serve as evidence.

In the 1950's, little girls across the country were subjected to *Toni* home perms at the hands of amateur family members. In short, *Toni* was a sinister permanent wave scheme that offered girls with long, straight hair, the option of curly ringlets. There was little to nothing in the instruction booklet about girls with *short*, straight hair and the possible issues that might arise a few hours into the process. But did that ambiguity deter the hundreds, perhaps thousands of hairdresser wannabes? No, it did not.

Of course, in later years, it made perfect sense to my mother and her sister, Maggie, that if *I* was getting a perm, my cousin Sherry would get one at the same time. Let's make it a family affair, they thought.

Short bangs were also permed, and the result was often staggering. Our mothers were so pleased—we were often horrified. There *were* those rare occasions that we actually resembled the cute little girls on the front of the *Toni* box. We never questioned the lack of consistency. Instead, there we sat, year after year, the two of us, in the garage with the door wide open for adequate ventilation, perched on kitchen chairs, with literally dozens of ½- inch, hard-plastic, pink and purple curler rods snapped firmly to our heads. The overpowering odor of the *Toni* solution permeated our sinuses as each curler rod was sufficiently saturated. It was just a given that no amount of plastic wrap or towels could keep the foul-smelling liquid from dripping down the back of our necks or into our ears. All for the sake of curls. Curls that we never asked for.

The upside? Fast forward. We survived to tell the story to our grandchildren.

Sweet Rosemary

―――᧶―――

*Her eyes told a story of pain and rejection,
but her hands possessed the creative gifting of an artist.*

She was in the third grade with me but was considerably older than the rest of my classmates. I was eight, and Rosemary was almost eleven. Her desk was right next to mine, and although she smiled often, her dark eyes told a story of pain, rejection, and disappointment.

Rosemary was very creative, and even as she struggled academically, she more than excelled in art. She gracefully brought life to a simple piece of paper with colored pencils and crayons. I was mesmerized by her artistic abilities. As it was, I helped her with spelling and math, and in return, she was quick to lend a seasoned hand with my art projects. We were a happy team.

I always enjoyed playing and talking with Rosemary during recess—and looked forward to sharing my lunch with her when the bell rang at noon. One day, I nonchalantly asked her, while we were munching on an apple, "Rosemary, why don't you bring *your* lunch to school?" Her countenance suddenly changed, and with her head down, she answered softly, "I'm usually not very hungry." I was much younger than Rosemary, but even I knew that didn't sound right—*my* stomach started growling in the classroom at 10:30 am! When I told Mom about my friend, Rosemary, she immediately started putting extra fruit and treats in my lunchbox for sharing.

Rosemary was usually very quiet in class and easily intimidated by Mrs. Johnson's raspy, cigarette-voiced commands to participate in group discussions. But she seemed to be more relaxed, even animated, on the playground with me. Over time, she became less shy, engaged more with other classmates, and happily shared my lunch every day.

I loved her sweet, tender ways and have often wondered through the years what ever happened to Rosemary. Be well, my dear friend. Be well.

Miss Boots

I knew in my heart that the Westbrook brothers were guilty, but nothing could change what they had done.

She was my sweet calico kitty, possessing just as many delightful ways as she did multi-colored patterns on her beautiful fur coat. Her four white boots made it all but easy to choose an appropriate name. I loved Miss Boots right from the beginning. Mom and Dad brought her home when she was just a kitten, and, as it was, she rarely left my side after that day. She slept at the foot of my bed on a bright pink blanket every night.

When Miss Boots was a little older, she would follow me halfway to school each day, then right back home, to keep Mom company while I was gone. She made it a point to be sitting on the porch to greet me in the afternoon.

Everybody loved Miss Boots, except Frank and John Westbrook, older boys who lived in the neighborhood. Both got BB guns for Christmas, and they delighted in taunting me with promises to use Miss Boots as target practice.

"You better leave Miss Boots and me alone, or I'll tell my dad!" I yelled, reasonably confident that the Westbrook boys wouldn't be a problem after a threat of that magnitude.

One day after school, I was surprised to find that Miss Boots was not sitting on the porch as usual. She wasn't in the house, so I searched the neighborhood, calling her name and asking neighbors if they had seen her. No one had. After about an hour of looking, I found her in an empty lot not far from our house. She was dead. Someone had shot and killed my sweet Miss Boots. The pain of losing her was immense for my seven-year-old heart, and I cried for days.

My dad embarked on a personal mission to find out who had done such a horrendous thing, but to no avail. Although their parents and mine questioned them, Frank and John Westbrook denied any involvement in Miss Boots' demise—but I knew better.

It was a long while before I could talk about Miss Boots without becoming emotional. In time, she became a very precious memory.

Color Them Magical

Aunt Maggie's creative and colorful touches transformed everything. Even Minnie Mouse stepped in style!

She is in all my earliest and fondest memories, a mere seventeen years older than me—my mama's baby sister, and *my* Aunt Maggie, how I love her!

One of my most memorable birthday gifts in December of 1959 was a giant Mickey Mouse coloring book. I could hardly wait for Aunt Maggie to color the first picture. She took her time selecting shades that were not typical for Minnie Mouse—but it didn't matter, because Minnie was about to experience a whole new magical, colorful world at the artistic hands of my Aunt Maggie.

She delighted in using all the colors in the big Crayola box—even the gold, silver, and copper shades in the back, which I often overlooked. She always created little hand-drawn accessories—necklaces, bracelets, earrings, and belts — for the characters "to spice things up."

When she wasn't coloring with crayons, Aunt Maggie was engrossed with paint-by-number creations that always looked far better than the image on the box. I'm more than certain that she substituted brighter, more colorful hues than what was suggested on the numbered canvases. Of course, the finished artwork was always stunning, with the inevitable touches of gold and silver. A true artist she is.

Dora Jane

Nothing could have prepared me for the heart stopping sight next to the tree on that festive Christmas morning.

Like all Christmas celebrations in my youth, the utter astonishment surrounding the holiday sights, smells, and tastes was nothing short of mesmerizing. Even at the seasoned age of nine, I was a devoted fan of the glorious holiday. However, nothing could have prepared me for the heart stopping sight standing next to the Christmas tree in our living room that festive morning in 1959.

For the sake of history, I first saw Dora Jane in the Sears Christmas catalog. She was undoubtedly the most beautiful doll I had ever seen! I marked the page where she and several of her three-foot-tall friends were wonderfully displayed. The incessant begging for Dora Jane began shortly after Thanksgiving dinner and continued over the next several weeks. Bless my parents for their endless patience.

The joy of meeting my new "friend" was truly unimaginable! I was ecstatic! In a flash, I envisioned countless adventures that awaited Dora Jane and me. Before Christmas, my sweet mama diligently labored at the sewing machine for several nights after I went to bed, creating an array of beautiful outfits for Dora Jane. She was destined to become the best-dressed doll in the whole world—well, at least in the neighborhood.

Dora Jane brought more happiness than any other Christmas gift I received over the years. She stood proudly in my bedroom until my early teens, with a little less hair, but very well loved.

Because of Goldie

To be fair, Mr. Ramsey warned us, but everyone said he was all talk—until the day he wasn't.

It was Christmas Eve of 1959, and my parents brought home an eight-week-old yellow lab puppy as a gift for our family. She was beautiful, and of course, we named her Goldie. She had one of the sweetest dispositions, and we all adored her.

Goldie was about five months old when we made the long trip from Vallejo, California, to our new home in Boise, Idaho. Everyone in the neighborhood loved Goldie—well, except for old Mr. Ramsey, who lived across the street in the big blue house on the corner. He made it abundantly clear that he didn't like dogs and that we had better keep Goldie away from his yard—or else. No one was entirely sure what Mr. Ramsey meant by "or else."

We had only lived in Boise for two weeks when Goldie managed to dig under the front yard fence and make her way across the street to the alley behind Mr. Ramsey's house. Sometime later, when we first noticed that she was gone, Dad whistled and called her name. She ambled out of the alley, in fact, stiffly. Dad knew that something was wrong and ran across the street to pick her up and carry her back to our yard. She convulsed violently, and there was no doubt what had occurred. Goldie had been poisoned. Even in her pain, her sweet temperament prevailed—she wagged her tail between convulsions.

Our veterinarian arrived at the house soon after and administered drugs to counter the effects of the poison. But it was too late. Goldie was gone. It was one of the first times I saw my dad cry. It was because of Goldie that we all cried.

Sweetpea

―⁓―

*She was gone in a flash,
and my heart broke at that same moment.*

She first captured my attention at J.J. Newberry, the famous five-and-dime variety store, where she sat perched with several of her chatty, colorful friends. The bright yellow parakeet seemed enamored with me and scurried from one end of the perch to the other to get a better look. A few days later, Mom surprised me with the little yellow parakeet and a bright blue cage. It was love at first sight, and clearly, mutual adoration existed between a happy nine-year-old and a young bird.

Sweetpea quickly adapted to her surroundings and kept a close eye on our whereabouts. She spent little time in her cage, preferring to be close to wherever there was human activity. She was notorious for following us outdoors and once flew off for several hours. We got the word out that she was missing, and thankfully, a neighbor spotted her in their backyard and returned her to a distraught little girl. Sweetpea never took flight outside again.

She loved playing on the floor with me and especially enjoyed scampering in and out of my two-story metal dollhouse. Sweetpea was equally mesmerized by the colorful plastic dollhouse furniture and busied herself with scattering the pieces around in the various rooms. She even became territorial when I handled any of the household contents and quickly made her displeasure known.

One Saturday morning, Sweetpea and I were happily playing on the living room floor with the dollhouse. Suddenly, unaware of Sweetpea's whereabouts, I crawled around to the backside of the house to look for her. In a flash, a misplaced knee became the catalyst for changing my world. "Daddy, fix her!" I screamed, staring in disbelief at Sweetpea's lifeless form. But this time, my hero daddy was as helpless as I. My head started to spin, and the instant grief that now threatened to consume me became nearly more than my young mind could grasp. How can this be? Life without Sweetpea was an unbearable thought.

It would be several years before I was interested in another parakeet. My heart still belonged to Sweetpea, and it felt like a betrayal of our special friendship to replace her. But, in time, there would be another that captured my attention—and eventually, my heart.

Yellow Roses

She was born on Flag Day, deeply rooted in Scientology, and an outspoken political activist. To me, Mrs. Long was my friend and fierce advocate—and that's all that mattered.

Pearl Long. She was our 80-year-old next-door neighbor, and we loved her dearly, especially me. She was overtly opinionated, deeply devoted to Scientology, an outspoken political activist, and an extraordinarily gifted artist. She was especially proud that her birthday was on Flag Day and quickly told you so, even if you hadn't asked.

When the 1960 movie "Pollyanna" premiered at the Egyptian Theatre in Boise, Idaho, Mrs. Long strolled to our front door and asked my mom if I might be allowed to accompany her to see the full-length feature. It was my first trip to a theatre, and I was beyond thrilled. Popcorn and orange soda only enhanced the already delightful experience.

Mrs. Long was a fabulous artist, and I can still see in my mind the many beautiful oil paintings displayed on the walls of her little house in the East End of Boise. She loved yellow roses and had a yard full of lovely, well-tended blooms. She also had what I considered a masterpiece still life of yellow roses in a pale green vase, which hung in her living room. I was awestruck by her artistic talent and creativity.

Beautiful French doors separated her kitchen from the living room area, and she had meticulously painted floral designs on each of the twenty-four glass panes. What a fascinating lady she was. Even at nine years old, I knew that I was in the presence of wisdom personified when I visited with her. She always greeted me at her front door in the same manner, "Well, hello there, little lady." Mrs. Long treated me with kindness, dignity, and respect—and conversed as though she was interested in every word I spoke. How I loved her!

I'll never forget the Saturday morning when my grandpa arrived at her house to begin construction on a backyard storage shed that would eventually house all her garden tools, water hoses, wheelbarrow, and push lawnmower. I sat on my blue swing set in *our* backyard, in full pout mode. Much to my utter dismay, Mom informed me earlier that I couldn't visit Grandpa while he was working next door at Mrs. Long's. It was painful to see them both talking and laughing and not be in the mix. Instead, I entertained childish fantasies of a potential blossoming love affair between the long-ago-widowed Mrs. Long and even longer-widowed Grandpa. Of course, it never happened. All that occurred was a well-built storage shed in her backyard several days later.

Pearl Long died shortly before I graduated from high school, and the world became just a little less interesting without her extraordinary artistic flair.

Clarence and Lena

Some described them as eccentric, childless, germophobe, busybodies—but they treated me like a princess, and I loved them both.

They were our delightfully eccentric next-door neighbors in East End Boise. She was thoroughly Scottish, and quite uninhibited by 1960s standards—especially in Idaho. He was a well-dressed businessman who worked at a downtown Boise men's clothing store and always smelled of tobacco and Old Spice aftershave. They had no children, but in a short while, considered me their own.

Lena kept an immaculate house, and Clarence tended their yard in like manner. They were both germophobes, and I was always fascinated by their continual handwashing and the faint scent of bleach in their kitchen. Now that I think of it, they must have been horrified that I routinely, and directly, drank water from our front yard water spicket during the sweltering summer months!

Lena knew literally everything about everybody. Wearing just her bra and a perfectly pressed mid-calf skirt, she'd lean her tiny frame against the white picket fence that separated our properties and happily educate all of us on the happenings in the neighborhood—and in the lives of its residents. Mom didn't care much for Lena's skimpy attire, especially when she was visiting with Dad at the fence. In those instances, it was a common sight for Mom to hightail out the front door, make the duo a threesome, and cut the conversation short. Although Clarence was more unassuming and less pretentious, I loved them both dearly and spent a great deal of time visiting at their house. The greeting at the front door was always the same: "Well, there's our little girl."

Because Lena was such a petite woman, her high-heeled shoes were a perfect fit for me. The day she decided to clean out her closet and downsize her shoe collection was a life-changing moment. She gave me several pairs to "play dress-up," as she put it. Although the fancy heels weren't necessarily the perfect accessories for my shorts and T-shirts, it didn't matter, and I wore them with pride. I even mastered riding my bicycle in high heels.

We were adequately informed of Clarence and Lena's upcoming trip to the Seattle World's Fair long before they departed for their week-long adventure in June 1962. They would go on to say—for years—that the Seattle World's Fair attracted 10 million visitors, of which they were two, during its six-month run. I was elated beyond belief when they presented me with a beautiful gold bracelet and 10 charms depicting sights from the 1962 Seattle World's Fair.

Throughout the years, they were dear neighbors, and even dearer souls. I'll never forget the day that Lena placed a small 10k gold ring in my hand, saying through tears, "This is my wedding ring, and I want you to have it. You're the daughter of my heart."

Lena cared for her beloved Clarence at home until he passed away at 88. She lived to celebrate her 100th birthday and meet my firstborn daughter.

Roosevelt Market

The little market was a gathering place for local neighbors and anyone else who happened to wander in looking for a smile and a cup of coffee. Even animals knew they were welcome.

I first visited the little neighborhood market in the spring of 1960. We had just moved from Vallejo, California, to the East End of Boise, Idaho, in April. I was enrolled in the third grade at Roosevelt Elementary School, which was situated directly across the street from the market. I knew that school would soon be out for summer vacation and already had plans to frequent the Roosevelt Market—especially when I caught sight of the penny candy showcase in the front area of the store, and the ice cream freezer in the back. My future was bright.

Established in 1900, the little neighborhood gathering place at 311 N. Elm Street was a full-service market in 1960. During those early days, my mom shopped exclusively at Roosevelt Market, claiming they had everything she needed—and that it was within walking distance, no less. Besides, according to Mom, George was an excellent butcher and ensured that she had the best cuts of meat. I loved being her helper and always enjoyed walking the two blocks to the market to purchase a pound of hamburger for $0.63, a loaf of bread for $0.22, and a roll of Smarties for a penny.

Dad had his own reasons for asking me to make a trip to the market and frequently gave me twenty-five cents on Saturday afternoon for ice cream and penny candy—with instructions to walk slowly, both ways. I knew exactly what *that* meant, too.

Saturday Morning Glory

*Waffles, bacon, gospel music, and
a Norwegian Grandpa.
It was a standard affair—but it never grew old.*

It was the same routine every Saturday morning, but, believe me, it never grew old. Really. The kitchen always smelled of waffles and warm maple syrup. Bacon sizzled in a cast-iron skillet on the stovetop. The wonderful aromas, along with gospel music blaring from the RCA stereo console, drew us all to the table for breakfast and happy conversation. Sometimes my grandpa would walk ten blocks from his house to ours and join us. He loved bacon, and I loved to hear him pray in Norwegian.

Household chores were a family affair, and everyone was involved, even the dog. Princess was our miniature black-and-tan dachshund. She learned very quickly that she could earn a special treat by gathering up our slippers and delivering them to their respective closets.

Mom always made cleaning and organizing fun. She would get a piece of colored paper and list all the chores to be tackled. Then, she would cut the paper into strips, fold them, and place them all in a round metal bowl. We would each take a folded piece with a corresponding task. Once the job was done, we'd take another strip, and so on until the bowl was empty. Before we knew it, the house was clean and tidy.

Of course, there was also yard work. Dad wasn't so much about making the task fun as just getting the job done. I loved working alongside my dad and being his helper. He mowed the grass, and I raked the clippings. Without a doubt, we were a good team.

Once all the indoor and outdoor chores were completed, Dad retreated to his workshop to delve into upholstery projects—Mom and I got dressed and walked to the corner to catch the bus to town. I had my allowance tucked away in my shiny, red purse—50 cents went a long way, even with 10 cents set aside for the church offering the following morning.

A trip into town usually meant lunch at the J. J. Newberry counter and then a little shopping in the store. Of course, it never failed that we would have our pictures taken—a long, narrow strip of four—in the little photo booth next to the lunch counter. I always got a small white sack filled with my favorite candy. Something was inevitably put on layaway for the start of school in September or for Christmas. Mom usually made a few small purchases: embroidery thread, crochet needles, and handkerchiefs for Dad.

After a stroll down the streets of town to do a little window shopping, we happily carried our treasures back onto the bus and headed for home. It had been another wonderful Saturday, with memories made that would last a lifetime and beyond.

Sunday Afternoon Drive

A frightening, overnight stay in a big, scary, two-story house became an anticipated, recurring weekend rendezvous.

Nearly every Sunday, rain or shine, we made the long road trip to visit my dad's Scandinavian family in Payette, Idaho. The old two-story house where his cherished aunt and uncle lived set back from the frontage road on a picturesque stretch of land, with a tree-lined dirt lane leading to the property. I first clambered up the front porch steps when I was just two years old.

Uncle Irvin never married but instead shared his life and lovely home with his sister, Anna, for over 35 years. He and Anna nurtured a beautiful flower garden every year, along with a huge vegetable garden. Irvin loved to take pictures and had countless photographs and slides. As a child, I would groan in disbelief when the slide projector and screen were removed from the hall closet and set up in the living room. Why were we about to see the same slides again? What could have changed since we saw them last? But, despite my inner questions (God forbid I would ever have considered voicing them), Irvin narrated the presentation as if we were viewing each slide for the very first time. In later years, I came to appreciate

Irvin's photographic talents and his remarkable recall of every detail of the image. He also owned and operated a small radio and television repair shop next to his home. I always knew that when our television or radio quit working for whatever reason, a trip to Irvin's shop would fix the problem. And it usually did. I loved Irvin. He was a gentle soul and truly found delight in his family and nature's beauty. I always remember him wearing a long-sleeved flannel shirt, regardless of the season.

Anna never married either, but instead gave her entire life to unselfish service, caring for family members —her mother, brothers, and nephews. She was a kind and compassionate person and always functioned in the "servant" mode, concerned foremost that everyone was taken care of and comfortable. I always wondered if Anna, so pretty and sweet, had ever claimed a genuine love of her own. And the answer I learned was 'yes,' she did. Dave Treen was a hired hand on her family's homestead in Nebraska. He quickly caught the eye of the farmer's daughter, and the two developed a close relationship that would have led to marriage. Fearful of this union and the impact it might have on the future caretaking role she had in mind for her eldest daughter, Anna's mother firmly objected to the continuation of a relationship with Dave. Faithful to her submissive nature, Anna forfeited this love and resigned herself to being forever single.

When I was about five years old, I recall another trip to their home. I was happy with what I believed was a short visit, but terrified when I found out we were spending the night in a big, scary, two-story house. Anna, even though she had no children of her own, had an uncanny way of making little people feel comfortable and at home. She called me into the kitchen and lifted me to the window so that I could see a white squirrel (the only albino squirrel I've seen since) outside in their front yard. I was totally enamored, and Anna was delighted with my childish excitement. I soon discovered that there were good things to eat at her house: cookies, ice cream, and lefse with butter and sugar.

Irvin passed away suddenly at the age of eighty-five. Anna was heartbroken at the loss of her brother, but, despite it, lived to celebrate 101 blessed years. They were both remarkable storytellers and tremendous influencers—my personal gateway to the past.

Rose of Remembrance

Carrie was taken away before we could bid farewell to each other, and there is a part of my heart that never fully reconciled with that reality.

We were best friends right from the start of the fourth grade at Roosevelt Elementary School in Boise, Idaho. It was September of 1962. We lived two blocks apart, so we walked to and from school every day.

I lived in a quaint yellow house shared with my parents, and she lived in a big gray building with lots of other children. Her parents had abandoned their five beautiful daughters a year before, and now she was a resident of the Idaho Children's Home. She always had a smile, her sweet face accentuated with deep dimples. But her soft, brown eyes told a far different story than her cheerful disposition. Carrie was well acquainted with sadness and loss.

Carrie's charming personality afforded her many opportunities for friendship. Teachers adored her. Despite attempts by classmates to befriend her, she was my shadow, staying close by my side. Carrie spent many weekends at our house and gravitated to my mother for the maternal affection she craved. I was always more than happy to share the blessings of my family and home life with her. She went to church with us frequently, and we even attended a weeklong summer camp together. Days were so much brighter with Carrie! She loved red roses, and Mom often cut a beautiful bloom from one of many bushes along our backyard fence to give to "her special girl."

Just before the start of fifth grade, Carrie tearfully informed me that a family from Texas was interested in adopting her. Unfortunately, their interest did not extend to Carrie's sisters, the youngest of whom was only two years old. We were both frightened at the prospect of her being taken away—especially to Texas—the distance sadly confirmed by our study of a United States map in the school library. I promised her that I would talk to my parents about adopting her so that she wouldn't have to move and live with people she didn't know. Neither of us was aware that the adoption process was well underway, and that we had very little time to spend together, or minimal say about her eventual destination.

A couple of days passed, and I walked to the Children's Home to see if Carrie could come to my house and play. A social worker met me at the front door and said that she was already gone. *What?* How could this be? The woman was nice enough, stating with some level of sympathy, "Debbie, you won't be able to write her or have any contact. Please remember the many good times you had with Carrie and wish her well." Carrie moved to Texas to start a new life, and mine felt like it was over. I cried all the way home.

I never had the chance to say goodbye to Carrie, and even after all these years, her absence still lingers in my heart. I often find myself thinking about the sweet, brown-eyed girl, hoping that life brought her all the happiness she so deeply deserved. For you, dear friend, a red rose of remembrance—a poignant reminder of our friendship and the love you shared with my family.

A Picnic in the Park

They were simply family get-togethers, filled with delicious food and lively conversation. Often, we chose to enjoy these gatherings in the park.

My memory bank is overflowing with happy childhood recollections during the summer season. Steeped in rich tradition, picnics were celebrated with enthusiasm, good food, and lots of family. There was peace that surrounded each gathering, a contentment that made you feel good to be part of a family with such great love and respect for one another.

Picnics were frequent, sometimes nothing more than putting a little of this and a little of that together and then making a run to a favorite park. Of course, there were those unique culinary creations that only individual family members could make; these were not to be messed with and were by no means replicated by anyone else. All but sacred, they were; Aunt Maggie's Banana Pudding and Strawberry Shortcake, Aunt Betty's Potato Salad, Mom's Baked Beans and Chocolate-Mayonnaise Cake, and Aunt Johanne's Macaroni Salad.

Uncle Floyd was the trusted grill master, ensuring that even a hot dog was cooked to perfection. Dad was the king of homemade ice cream. Grandpa didn't let too much time go by before he threw out a challenge to play a game or two of horseshoes.

When it got dark, fireflies became magical night fairies tempting us with "catch us if you can." We played game after game of hide and seek—until we nearly dropped from exhaustion. But even then, a glass of sweet tea or red Kool-Aid was the fuel needed to start all over again. Adult conversations and laughter continued late into the evening, creating lasting memories of warmth and happiness.

The Upholstery Bus

―››‹‹―

Connie Francis crooning in the background, Paul Harvey wrapping up another "rest of the story" and the steady hum of a commercial sewing machine.

Two Saturday mornings a month during the summer, my bedroom door swung open to my dad's welcome call to action, "It's time to get up, Debbie. We have a long road to travel, and we need an early start." In no time, I was dressed, carrying a light pack and go breakfast, and out the front door—only to run back and hug Mom goodbye.

Our first stop was City Upholstery in downtown Boise—Dad's place of work. He operated the customized 40-foot red-and-white upholstery bus, and twice a month, Dad became the famed "Upholstery Guy" in Fruitland, Idaho. It was a 110-mile round-trip, and I was his honorary, highly compensated assistant. Fifty cents a day was a good wage for a ten-year-old. My job description was simple: make runs to the little drive-in next to the parking lot, and keep the bus floor free of fabric scraps, and the like. The small oscillating fan kept us cool in the sweltering 100-degree summer heat—cold lemonade with extra ice helped, too.

In conjunction with my regular job as errand girl and janitor, by mid-summer, Dad expanded my title to junior apprentice. In short, I was on my way to learning the upholstery business. With a few basic sewing skills under my belt and the ability to easily identify upholstery tools and gadgets, Dad had the assurance that I was more than ready to operate the adding machine and make change. We were a team.

Then there was the need for a pleasant work environment. The remedy? A brown RCA Radiola 61-8 AM radio was placed on a shelf, always on, so Dad never missed Connie Francis singing a few numbers. It never failed that he remarked, after each song, "Boy, she has a nice voice." Of course, Connie Francis was one of the top-charting female vocalists of the late 1950s and early 1960s. She sold over one hundred million records, placing her among the best-selling music artists in history. Dad didn't care about all that. He just loved to hear her sing "Who's Sorry Now."

When Connie wasn't crooning another "somebody done somebody wrong song," Paul Harvey was broadcasting *The Rest of the Story*, which consisted of true accounts, most often forgotten, based on a variety of subjects, with some key element of the story (generally the name of a well-known person) withheld until the end. The broadcasts always concluded with a variation on the tag line, "And now you know... the *rest* of the story."

At the end of a long day, tired though we may have been, it was another good one for the books. Such wonderful memories of summer days spent with my dad. And now you know, the *rest* of the story.

Good as Gold

S&H Green Stamps: the gateway to an entire world of possibility.

In the heart of the 1960s, our family's kitchen table was more than a place for meals—it was the headquarters for a quiet, thrilling enterprise. S&H Green Stamps, those little rectangles of promise, were the currency of dreams in our household. Mom was the mastermind, her eyes lighting up each time she returned from the grocery store with a fresh batch of stamps tucked inside her purse. She'd hand them to me with a smile, and I'd get to work, carefully licking the backs and pressing them into the pages of her coveted booklets. The glue tasted terrible, but the anticipation was sweet.

The S&H catalog was our window to possibility. On rainy afternoons, Mom and I would sit together, flipping through its glossy pages, imagining the treasures we might one day claim. Toasters, blenders, picnic sets, and even bicycles—each item seemed just within reach, if only we could fill enough booklets. Sometimes, we'd circle our favorites with a blue ballpoint pen, making plans for the future as if we were plotting a grand adventure.

Mom was vigilant about her stamps. If the cashier at the market forgot to include them in the grocery bag, she'd send me back with a polite but determined request. "Excuse me, but we didn't get our Green Stamps," I'd say, clutching the receipt in one hand and hope in the other. The clerks always obliged, handing over the precious stamps with a knowing smile. It was a small victory, but it felt enormous.

Dad, too, was drawn into the Green Stamp mission. Whenever he filled the tank at the gas station, he'd make sure to ask for his stamps before leaving. "Don't forget the Green Stamps!" he'd remind the attendant, as if the fate of our household depended on it. In a way, it did. Those stamps were more than just a reward for shopping—they were as good as gold.

As the booklets filled, we'd count the pages together, calculating how close we were to the next big prize. The day we finally redeemed our stamps for a beautiful brass lamp for our living room was a celebration. We gathered around the shiny new addition, admiring our hard-earned reward, and savoring the sense of accomplishment.

Looking back, those Green Stamps were worth far more than their face value. They were the glue that held together countless afternoons of laughter, planning, and togetherness. In the currency of memory, they remain priceless.

The Porch Light

It was an unspoken rule, a language that kids of summer knew all too well— when it was time to head home.

Let me tell you, if I *ever* had any thought of jeopardizing the blessed freedom I had been afforded due to my trustworthy nature, it was swiftly banished from my mind. I loved running the neighborhood in the summertime, and I knew how to keep it that way. It was easy. Pay attention to simple instructions and watch for the porch light to come on when it got dark. Nothing else was quite so important in my young life. I already had it down about strangers and looking both ways before crossing the street.

These were the days long before the introduction of cell phones, so it was imperative to remember what you were supposed to do before you left the house. It really wasn't that difficult. Usually, it was to be home in time for dinner. That left the entire day for a myriad of fun times.

Most of my summer escapades involved a friend or two who lived nearby, and our adventures were endless. We especially loved riding our bikes and screaming to the top of our lungs as the neighborhood dogs chased us down the street. Everyone had a dog, but none of them were even remotely purebred. In fact, the majority of the dogs in the neighborhood were related to each other. When we got tired and hot, we'd stop for a drink of water from a neighbor's water hose and a quick run through their sprinklers. Of course, we'd always make our way to Roosevelt Market for a popsicle and some penny candy before riding to the community pool—we had our swimsuits and plastic swim caps in our bicycle baskets. After several hours of swimming and jumping off the high dive, we'd ride to the school playground for a while before heading home. According to the watch I got for Christmas the year before, it was almost time for dinner—and I wasn't about to be late.

After dinner, and once the dishes were washed and dried, there was more playing outside. Fireflies, hide and seek, and sips of water from the hose. Finally, I'd see it. The porch light came on, and I knew exactly what it meant.

Friends exchanged goodbyes and promised more adventures the next day. Ah, childhood memories of summer.

Roughing It

Our 13-foot travel trailer became the gateway to a world packed with adventure and endless possibilities.

"Coffee, anyone?" Mom loved camping, and our little travel trailer proved to be one of the most enjoyable means of "roughing it". She often said that it was the most fun she ever had!

Dad surprised her one afternoon in early summer of 1961 with the 13' Aristocrat Lil' Loafer. When he pulled slowly into the driveway with the little trailer attached to the back of his red Ford pickup, Mom was ecstatic. Over the next few days, she began packing it with everything (and I do mean *everything*) we'd need for our first trip to Birch Creek, a favorite campsite next to the Payette River and under the tall, Idaho pines. Even our dachshund, Candy, was excited, especially when she saw her small wicker bed loaded into the trailer.

The following Friday evening, when Dad came home from work, we happily headed to Birch Creek in Lowman, Idaho, for the weekend. By the time we finally arrived, it was getting dark. First things first, once the trailer was parked between two towering pines, Dad hung the old Coleman lantern from a low-hanging branch to illuminate our space. In eagerness to check out the campsite,

Candy began running around with her nose close to the ground. Oblivious to the fact that she was close to the river's edge, she inadvertently tumbled into the fast-moving current. Dad ran alongside the bank and finally retrieved the terrified, wet dog from the river. Candy stayed close to the trailer and her wicker bed, following the near-catastrophic incident.

When the first rays of sunlight filtered through the trailer curtains the next morning, we were up and ready to begin a fun-filled day. The aroma of pancakes on the griddle, bacon frying in a small cast-iron skillet, and fresh-brewed coffee on the back burner of the little green stovetop stirred our appetites. Mom placed a red-and-white checkered tablecloth on the picnic table, and we all wholeheartedly agreed that everything tasted better outdoors.

After breakfast, and before too much time had passed, Dad and I made our way to a large boulder near the river's edge that was the perfect place to sit and drop our fishing lines. Repeatedly, we felt the tug on the line and the bend of the pole as one large rainbow trout after the other was pulled from the fast-moving water. Once we reached our limits, we headed back to the trailer. Dinner was fabulous!!

At day's end, a trip to a nearby hot springs for a relaxing soak was all we needed for a restful sleep. Even in later years, Mom always said that camping at Birch Creek held some of her fondest memories. Of course, I agree.

Coming of Age

―❦―

A new season, a new beginning,
A new awareness.

Growing up was both exhilarating and anxiety-producing. I often felt like the little prairie dog that routinely sticks its head out of its underground burrow to cautiously look around and survey the unknown landscape. It can choose to scamper about and explore—or quickly disappear to a place of safety and refuge when it's had enough. Thankfully, my parents allowed me to navigate the inevitable passage from childhood to young adulthood at my own pace.

Cherish the Days
Cherish the days, for the time will come.
When childhood fades, like the setting sun.
Seasons come, and seasons go.
The birth of spring, and summer's glow
Autumn arrives with its golden red hues,
Then comes winter.
~ D. L. Norris

The Day I Became a Woman

Who knew that the arrival of a brown papered package from Speigel had the potential to alter my world in such a manner.

It was a warm Saturday morning in the summer of 1962. I sat at the kitchen table as a happy, flat-breasted twelve-year-old, eating pancakes with my family, and talking about the imminent arrival of my California cousins. I was overjoyed. Later in the day, we planned to gather for a mini family reunion and a long-anticipated picnic near the Payette riverfront in the Idaho mountains. My swimsuit, towel, and tanning lotion were already packed in my bag—they *had* been for nearly a week.

All was about to change in a heartbeat. Shortly before noon, our mail carrier delivered a sizeable brown package from Spiegel that became the catalyst for thrusting me into womanhood. Who could have predicted that a sun hat and a heavily padded bra—my first—could alter my world in such a manner? But it most certainly did. I quickly tore open the package, admired the life-changing contents, and then spent a good two hours modeling in front of the bathroom mirror. Without a doubt, I was quite pleased with my new pre-teen figure.

As expected, my cousins arrived at our house in boisterous fashion, anxiously looking for me. "Where's Debbie?" they hollered. At the sound of their immature voices, I sauntered out of my bedroom, sporting a 36B bustline and a wide-brimmed sunhat. Of course, they were stunned. Dad's coffee cup nearly slipped from his grasp.

The thirty-mile drive to our favorite picnic area was long and without much conversation. It didn't matter. I had no intention of giving up my rite of passage without a fight. I sat proudly in the back seat of our 1957 Pontiac between my two silent cousins. Pam pouted the entire distance. Jan kept staring at my chest.

Once we arrived, I offered to help the other ladies with table setting, and the womanly task of arranging food. Of course, I would be sitting at the adult table, straight-backed, and with a napkin on my lap. The "kids" sat on folding lawn chairs, balancing paper plates on their knees.

"You look ridiculous," snarled Pam, as she brushed past me on her way to get more potato chips. "I suppose you're planning on wearing that dumb hat all day?"

I didn't have time for childish prattle. I was a woman now. Turning my attention to my Aunt Betty, I asked, "Would it be possible to get your recipe for the potato salad? It's absolutely delicious." My cousins moaned in disbelief and meandered off to gather pinecones.

As providence dictated, the afternoon temperatures were on a steady rise, and with it, my discomfort and boredom. I watched from the adult picnic table as the girls cooled off along the river's edge. They were laughing, jumping from big rocks into the water, and having what appeared to be a wonderful time. My new bra was scratchy. I was sweating. I didn't know if I could endure another story starting with, "Did I ever tell you about—"

Suddenly, I excused myself from a conversation about a crocheted doily and hurried to the picnic site outhouse with my tote bag. There I stripped down to my twelve-year-old, flat-breasted body once again, tossing the new bra and big sun hat in the bag. Slipping into my ruffled-bottomed, polka-dot swimsuit and pink flip flops, I made an enthusiastic bolt for the river. It never felt so good to be a kid.

Thirteen Chicks

―❦―

It all started with a school carnival and a game of ring toss. When it was all over, I was the proud owner of a box full of hatchlings.

The annual school carnival was on the calendar and definitely not an event to be missed. Even though I was no longer a student at Roosevelt Elementary, it didn't matter. The carnival also drew neighborhood residents, and thus, a few former students, me included, planned to attend and support our *alma mater*. We were now seasoned 12-year-olds at East Junior High School but still enjoyed a good neighborhood carnival once in a while.

True to carnival nature, there were a variety of games, attractive prizes, and lots of good food. I was especially taken with a game of Ring Toss that offered the potential to win baby chickens. Somehow, I got lost in the thrill of the game and ended up with a box full of fluffy yellow chicks—thirteen in all.

Mom and Dad weren't *nearly* as impressed as I. Dad spoke up first. "What do you intend to do with a bunch of chickens in the city?" he challenged, keeping a steady gaze on me. Well, that was a good question—and not one that I had fully considered. Nonetheless, in the interim, we got some chicken feed and kept them warm under a heat lamp. They thrived, of course. In no time, they were running about the backyard, free range.

It didn't take long before Dad came up with the idea that the half-grown chickens were better suited for farm life. His sister and family lived on a large dairy farm in rural Emmett, Idaho, about thirty-five miles from Boise, and that's where the chickens were headed, unbeknownst to them. It was a miserable car trip, primarily because the chickens were restless, and refused to remain in the box.

Several weeks later, we were invited for dinner with the family in Emmett. Fried chicken and potato salad were on the menu. No one made eye contact with each other at the table, and I dared not ask what I already knew.

Squirrel Blues

*Church and Jimmy Bowman would have to wait.
I had squirrel matters to tend to.*

We were on our way to church, all three of us dressed to the nines. I was thirteen, wearing my first pair of low-heeled shoes — black patent, no less — and sporting a new outfit from the Sears catalog that had arrived the day before. My hair was perfectly styled, and I was definitely feeling good about myself—even wondering if Jimmy Bowman might be attending church services on this fine Sunday morning.

There we stood on the stone walkway, enjoying a little small talk and much-needed shade under a tall elm tree in our yard. Dad mentioned driving the Pontiac around to the front of the house. Mom said that I looked nice in my new dress. I smiled and thanked her for the compliment. Suddenly, I felt a big "splat" on the top of my head. Looking up, I saw him sitting there, contentedly, on a large, overhanging branch—a fat, brown squirrel that had pretty well ruined my plans for church attendance and seeing Jimmy Bowman. Tears quickly formed in my eyes. Dad tried to be sympathetic, but I could tell he was having a tough time keeping a straight face. Even Mom was struggling.

Long story short, I went directly to the shower. Mom started dinner. Dad took off his suit and tie. We weren't going *anywhere*.

Transformative Years

Culturally, it was an era of upheaval, revolution, and achievement. For me, it was a mood-swinging, ever-challenging period—literally.

The 1960s represented a rapidly changing era of political upheaval, cultural revolution, and landmark achievements in science, art, and civil rights, leaving a lasting impact on American society and global history. The fast-moving *era* was not the only thing marked by significant change. My emotions were often like those of a roller coaster. Dad said I had an attitude. Mom more aptly identified the varying mood swings as "pre-period." *Whatever.* Growing up was challenging. Period.

GOODBYE, GRANDPA

I was thirteen, and the sudden loss of my 81-year-old grandfather was immense—partly because it was my first experience with the death of a family member—but mostly because I would miss him terribly. He was a big part of my young life, a constant presence in my world. I loved that he always treated me as a mini-adult, worthy of a cup of strong, black coffee whenever he was pouring. He was known to have a stash of candy in his shirt pocket and delighted in tossing a piece to me from across the room. He was a bacon enthusiast, but cooked onions were his worst enemy. He had no teeth, but it didn't matter. His broad smile and hearty laugh were infectious. The absence of teeth never seemed to hinder his ability to eat a crisp apple or chew a handful of salted peanuts. Grandpa had a million stories, many of which I had heard numerous times before. Still, I never ceased to listen, because his animated way of narrating events of the past always captured my attention, and my heart.

He walked, fast-paced, everywhere, and was the trusted neighborhood handyman. For the elderly person who was unable, he happily raked their lawns in the fall. He shoveled snow from their sidewalks in the winter. If a house or outbuilding needed a fresh coat of paint, he was the first to volunteer his services. If you needed something built, his carpentry skills were stellar. Whatever was broken, he knew how to fix it. How I loved him—and now he was gone.

Death of a President

I remember November 22, 1963, as though it were yesterday—a day forever etched in the collective memory of a nation. Mr. Beaumont, my seventh-grade American history teacher, had just snapped our rowdy class to order, instructing us to settle down, open our textbooks, and prepare to take notes. The ordinary hum of classroom life was suddenly interrupted when a special announcement came over the intercom, its tone urgent and somber. President John F. Kennedy, while traveling with a motorcade through downtown Dallas, Texas, had been mortally wounded by assassin Lee Harvey Oswald.

The gravity of the news swept through our classroom like a cold wind, silencing even the most restless students. We sat in stunned disbelief, struggling to comprehend how such a tragedy could unfold in real time. The assassination of President Kennedy was a shock that reverberated through every household, regardless of age or political persuasion. Later that afternoon, Vice President Lyndon B. Johnson was sworn into office, his oath a solemn reminder of the fragility of leadership and the abruptness with which history can change course. The sense of uncertainty lingered, deepened by the surreal events that followed—two days later, Oswald himself was shot and killed on live national television by Jack Ruby. This act only compounded the nation's grief and confusion.

Though my parents had not voted for John F. Kennedy, his assassination left them deeply shaken. I watched my mother shed quiet tears as she ironed my dad's shirts, the television flickering in the background. The voice of CBS News anchor Walter Cronkite delivered the devastating news with a gravity that made the moment feel both intimate and monumental. It was as if time itself had paused, allowing the world to mourn together. The sorrow transcended political boundaries; for those hours and days, the nation was united in grief, disbelief, and a profound sense of loss.

LIKE A CHAMELEON

What can I say? It was the absolute rage in the seventh grade. Of course, I needed to participate in whatever was considered "cool" at the moment. The rage, I speak of? A green, long-tailed, buggy-eyed, very much alive lizard (commonly referred to as a chameleon) that wore a small collar/leash made of embroidery thread was indeed the source of the rage.

All leashes were to be secured, not only to the lizard but to the shirt or sweater of the lizard owner. These were the rules, as outlined by the exasperated school administration. Obviously, they soon discovered that students and lizards outnumbered them, and concessions had to be made.

Most lizards were well-behaved in the classroom, and therefore, disruptions were rare. Of course, there were those occasional, unfortunate situations whereby a lizard happened to escape the embroidery noose and enjoy unfettered freedom about the classroom. Now that's another story; one involving the near-fatal cardiac episode of English teacher, Mrs. Donovan.

My lizard's name was Marsha. She was good-natured and easy to care for, whether at home or at school. No issues. That is, until one Saturday afternoon, she orchestrated a brazen get away from her glass, terrarium-style enclosure. Long story short, we never found Marsha. Mom was sure that she had disappeared through a floor vent and was living—*and* growing—in the crawl space under the house.

Long Hair and Liverpool

A truly historic moment unfolded on the evening of February 9, 1964—one that would forever alter the landscape of music, youth culture, and even the way families gathered around their televisions. That night, the Beatles, the electrifying rock band from Liverpool, made their legendary debut on The Ed Sullivan Show. Over seventy million viewers—more than a third of the American population at the time—tuned in, their anticipation palpable in living rooms across the country. Our household was no exception.

I remember the scene vividly: Mom and Dad settled comfortably on the sofa, their green jadeite coffee cups in hand, and their expressions a mixture of curiosity and skepticism. At the same time, I sat cross-legged on the carpet in front of the Magnavox television console—barely able to contain my excitement. As Ed Sullivan introduced the "four young men from Liverpool," the room fell silent.

The Beatles burst onto the screen—John, Paul, George, and Ringo—each with their signature mop-top haircuts and infectious energy. The audience's screams nearly drowned out the music, but nothing could diminish the impact of those opening chords. I was instantly mesmerized, my eyes glued to Paul McCartney, whose boyish charm and melodic voice made my teenage heart race.

Dad, ever the traditionalist, mumbled under his breath, "Good Lord, I wonder if they've ever had a decent haircut?" His tone was half-amused, half-bewildered, as if he couldn't quite decide whether to be concerned or entertained by this new phenomenon. Mom, with her characteristic wit, chimed in, "Or just a haircut, period—good *or* bad!"

For me, that night marked the beginning of a lifelong love affair with music and the magic of possibility. The Beatles weren't just a band; they were a cultural tidal wave, ushering in a new era of creativity. Their music became the soundtrack of my youth. That unforgettable night in our living room remains etched forever in my memory.

TRANSISTOR RADIOS

The arrival of the transistor radio marked a turning point not only in technology, but in the very fabric of youth culture. Compact, portable, and affordable, these little devices gave young people a newfound sense of independence, a private gateway to music, news, and ideas, all without the watchful eyes or ears of parents. For the first time, teenagers could tune in to their favorite stations, listen to the latest hits, and share in the excitement of cultural movements that were sweeping across the country. The transistor radio became a symbol of freedom, self-expression, and the growing influence of youth in society.

I remember the thrill of owning my own radio—a bright red Global GR 711, complete with a sturdy brown leather carrying case. It wasn't just an accessory; it was a constant companion, faithfully traveling with me wherever I went. Whether I was riding my bike through the neighborhood, picnicking at the park, or simply daydreaming in my room, the radio was always by my side, filling the air with the sounds of the Beatles and the Beach Boys, among others.

Of course, there *were* boundaries. My beloved radio was welcome almost everywhere—except church. That was the rule. On Sunday mornings, it stayed at home, while I joined my family in the pews. In all honesty, there was a reason why it was a rule in the first place, its genesis several Sunday's before during the singing of hymn, "How Great Thou Art." Simultaneously, Mom's keen sense of hearing picked up the faint song, "Good Vibrations," by the Beach Boys coming from my red purse. Needless to say, the Beach Boys never attended our church again.

Go-Go Boots

In 1966, the world was swept up in the infectious beat of Nancy Sinatra's hit song, "These Boots Are Made for Walkin'." With her iconic go-go boots and confident swagger, Sinatra didn't just popularize fashion trends, she ignited a movement. Suddenly, go-go boots were everywhere: in department store windows, on television, and most importantly, on the feet of teenagers like me who were eager to make a statement of their own.

As fifteen-year-old ninth-graders, my friends and I embraced the go-go boot craze with unrestrained enthusiasm. We wore our shiny white boots with pride, strutting down Hillside Junior High School hallways in unified mass. For us, the boots were more than just fashion accessories. They were a symbol of youthful independence, all the while giving us the sense that we were part of something bigger than ourselves.

I Have a Dream

Martin Luther King Jr. was an American Baptist minister, civil rights activist, and political philosopher who became a central figure in the civil rights movement from 1955 until his assassination in 1968. Through his unwavering commitment to nonviolent resistance and civil disobedience, King championed the advancement of civil rights for people of color in the United States, courageously confronting Jim Crow laws, and other forms of legalized discrimination.

King's leadership was pivotal during the 1963 March on Washington, where he delivered his iconic "I Have a Dream" speech on the steps of the Lincoln Memorial. He also played a key role in organizing the historic Selma to Montgomery marches in 1965, which were instrumental in the fight for voting rights. The civil rights movement, under King's guidance and inspiration, achieved landmark legislative victories, including the Civil Rights Act of 1964, the Voting Rights Act of 1965, and the Fair Housing Act of 1968.

As a junior at Capital High School in Boise, Idaho, I vividly recall when the news of Martin Luther King's assassination was announced. The impact was profound—many of us were deeply moved and saddened by his death. However, I also distinctly remember a disturbing number of classmates—and a few of my instructors—who expressed sentiments about the assassination that left me feeling cold inside.

Moon Landing

The first landing on the Moon represents one of humanity's most awe-inspiring achievements. On July 20, 1969, during NASA's historic Apollo 11 mission, astronauts Neil Armstrong and Buzz Aldrin became the first humans to set foot on the lunar surface. The world watched in collective anticipation as Armstrong descended the ladder of the lunar module, his every movement broadcast to over half a billion viewers worldwide. At precisely 10:56 p.m., Armstrong planted his boot on the powdery surface and uttered the immortal words: "That's one small step for a man, one giant leap for mankind."

I remember the moment clearly—the hush that fell over our living room as my family gathered around the television screen. The Moon, once a symbol of mystery and unreachable yearning, became a testament to human ingenuity, courage, and perseverance.

What many may not realize is that Armstrong carried with him a tangible link to the past: pieces of wood and fabric from the Wright brothers' pioneering airplane, which first achieved powered flight in 1903—sixty-six years before Apollo 11's lunar landing. By bringing these relics to the Moon, Armstrong honored the extraordinary progress made in aviation and space exploration.

The Apollo 11 mission was the culmination of years of tireless effort and scientific innovation. It was a moment that inspired millions to look up at the night sky and believe that anything was possible.

The Great Escape

A motorcycle police chase was not something I ever considered —until now.

Well, it seemed like a promising idea at the time. But it sure didn't end well. It was the summer of 1968, and it all started with a Honda 90 Trail bike that my dad bought at Carl's Cycle Sales in Boise, Idaho. The bike usually traveled in the back of the Ford pickup and accompanied us on weekend jaunts to the mountains. Dad let me ride it a few times but always kept a close eye on my whereabouts and how I maneuvered his prized possession.

On this particular day, I convinced Dad that he could trust me to take the motorcycle for a road spin and bring it back in one piece. I guess I got lost in the moment; wind in my hair, sun on my back, and the care-free days of summer. I didn't even think to check the speedometer as I sailed past the officer sitting alongside the road in a grove of trees.

Sirens and flashing lights. Of course, in hindsight, I should have pulled the bike over immediately. But I had recently seen the feature film "Coogan's Bluff" with

Clint Eastwood, and the motorcycle chase was nothing short of exhilarating. Now, faced with a decision, a full-blown chase of my own seemed a plausible alternative to surrender. Besides, even though I had a valid driver's license, wouldn't you know I inadvertently left the house without my identification? Obviously, I had no choice.

I tore through the Chevron gas station and then whipped around the back of the Hawkin's Pac Out restaurant. Skidding to an abrupt stop, I found myself eye to eye with the exasperated officer. My short, adrenaline-charged life of crime was over. Of course, he was poised for a stern reprimand on the ills of alluding a peace officer. I even tried to throw Clint Eastwood under the bus, but to no avail. The officer didn't mention incarceration, but my mind had already raced ahead to contemplate the dismal possibility. My punishment, you ask? I was instructed to "walk" the Honda Trail bike the 3.08 miles to the front door of our house.

A worse fate awaited my arrival—Dad was standing in the doorway, and he wasn't happy. Let's just say that it was a long while before there were any more jaunts on the Honda 90 Trail bike. But I swear I saw a smile on my dad's face as he rolled it into the garage.

Days of Promise

Hopes, Dreams, and Life's Lessons

These were days brimming with hope, dreams, and anticipation. It was a time of new beginnings, but also inevitable endings. Joy was abundant, yet sadness sometimes arrived without forewarning. Looking back, it was simply the age-old journey of growing up—a path marked by both excitement and disappointment, ultimately shaping who I was destined to become.

A Gentle, Steady Stream
Time, a gentle, steady stream,
Carries us far from what once seemed—
Endless summers, simple bliss,
Childhood laughter we dearly miss.
We trade our innocence, though not with regret,
Left with memories, we will not soon forget.
~ D. L. Norris

Rose-Colored Glasses

*Carefree days, and a rose-colored
view of everything around me.
Of course, that was destined to change.*

The 1970s unfolded as a dynamic era marked by political turbulence, sweeping cultural change, and significant breakthroughs in science, the arts, and civil rights. These transformative years profoundly shaped American society and resonated across the globe. For me, though, the turbulence of the times felt distant. I had just stepped into my twenties, and everything seemed bathed in a soft, rose-colored glow, no matter what was happening beyond the horizon. Life was carefree and exciting: I cruised around in a cherry-red 1972 Volkswagen convertible, surrounded by good friends and carried by a sense of infinite freedom. In those moments, it was easy to believe that life was truly as good as it seemed.

CLOSE TO YOU

The Carpenters, an iconic American duo comprised of siblings Karen and Richard Carpenter, captivated audiences with their signature blend of soft pop melodies and heartfelt harmonies. Karen's rich alto voice, paired with Richard's masterful arrangements and harmonizing, created a sound that was both instantly recognizable and profoundly moving. Over their 14-year career, the

Carpenters released ten albums and numerous singles and appeared in several memorable television specials. Among their many beloved songs, "Close to You" stands out as a personal favorite. This timeless love ballad marked their breakthrough in 1970 and solidified their place in music history.

John Boy

I truly believed I was in love—although, looking back, I'm not so sure. At the time, nothing could have convinced me otherwise. He was two years older, a good-looking, guitar-playing college student, while I was fresh out of high school, swept up in a whirlwind of hopes, dreams, and promises that made my head spin. In hindsight, the warning signs were there—I didn't want to see them and refused to listen. He left, supposedly for a brief visit with family in another state. But, as fate orchestrated, he never returned. And just like that, the short story ended.

Traveling Road Show

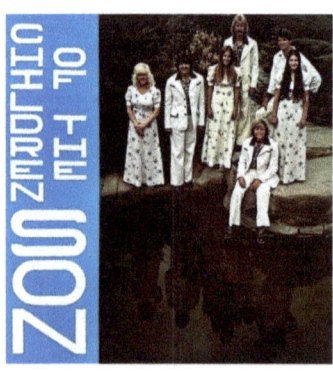

In the early 1970s, the West Coast gospel music group "Children of the Son" came together and soon after embarked on cross-country tours in a customized Greyhound bus. For my dad, this was nothing short of a nightmare, especially since the band members sported long hair, and he was still slowly coming to terms with the Beatles! Our "music with a beat" traveled with us in the form of record albums, 8-tracks, and cassettes, filling our heads with dreams that our name, "Children of the Son," might someday appear in flashing lights. As it was, the only flashing lights we saw were oncoming vehicles during the long bus trip back home.

We performed everywhere: churches, high schools, outdoor festivals, and even shared the stage with the Oak Ridge Boys back when their repertoire was strictly gospel—long before "Elvira" became a household hit.

In the spring of 1975, I married the lead singer of the group, and from there it was the blending of voices and lives that spanned nearly three decades—music, travel, laughter, tears, dreams, and two sweet babies. Of course, there was great sadness when the song ended.

Unexpected Blessing

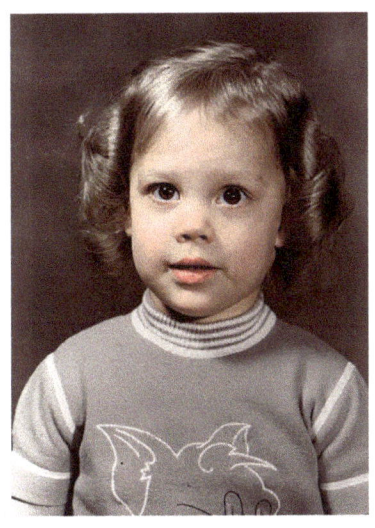

The news came as a shock to all. Especially me. After twenty years of holding the uncontested title of "only child," Mom shared the earth-shattering news at the breakfast table. She was pregnant. I was shocked and nearly choked on my biscuit. Dad almost fell off his chair. Trying to make small talk, while processing the unexpected announcement, I questioned (albeit cautiously), "Do women actually *have* babies at age 46?" Mom patiently explained that her obstetrician discussed the pregnancy in detail and assured her that there was no reason why she couldn't carry and deliver a healthy baby at her age. Dad's question wasn't as well-received, and as soon as the words fell out of his mouth, I knew he had skated out on thin ice. "Weren't you supposed to be paying attention to things like this?" Even the oxygen left the room. Like a bear charging out of its den, Mom was quick to set the record straight. "Well, I hardly did this on my own!" she snapped.

Once the air cleared, we finished breakfast and exchanged wary but happy smiles. Over the next several weeks, excitement steadily built, and plans were set in motion for the new arrival of "what's his name."

Fast forward, Robyn Ann was one of the greatest gifts ever to grace our family. My little sister made her debut on Friday, February 25, 1972, and the world hasn't been quite the same since.

Watergate

The nation watched in disbelief as President Richard Nixon, facing almost certain impeachment and conviction over the Watergate scandal, became the first U.S. president in history to resign from office on August 9, 1974.

The gravity of the moment settled over our household like a heavy blanket—you could have heard a pin drop as the news unfolded on the television. For a long moment, we sat in stunned silence, absorbing the enormity of what had just transpired. Then, breaking the tension, Dad finally spoke up, his voice echoing the bewilderment felt across the country: "Oh, for crying out loud, what in the world was he thinking?"

Jaws

It was June 20, 1975, and when Steven Spielberg's *Jaws* premiered in American theaters, it didn't just make waves—it created a tidal shift in movie history. The suspenseful tale of a great white shark terrorizing a small beach town quickly became a cultural phenomenon. Suddenly, everyone was talking about the film, and its haunting theme music.

For those of us who saw it that summer, the impact was immediate and unforgettable. The mere mention of *Jaws* was enough to send a chill down your spine, and the idea of swimming in lakes—or even venturing too far from the shore—became a source of genuine anxiety. That year, the water was quieter than ever, as children and adults alike hesitated before diving in, casting wary glances at the surface and imagining what might lurk beneath.

Night Stalker

*As a serial killer terrorizes a city,
a young woman wonders if she's his next victim.*

My bedroom windows rattled, and I was suddenly awakened from a deep sleep by what sounded like a massive explosion. With my heart racing, I jumped out of bed, quickly dressed in the darkness, and ran downstairs to peer out the front door. A huge fire had erupted two blocks away in an old, abandoned warehouse, and now the otherwise quiet neighborhood was overrun with curious spectators. The once-still night filled with the scream of sirens. Without thinking, I locked the door behind me and started walking toward the flaming building, joining others as we watched the scene unfold. It was a decision that would have dire consequences—and haunt me for a better part of my life.

The little one-bedroom, partially furnished apartment was a first, and had been my home for nearly five months. Located in the beautiful, tree-lined North End of Boise, Idaho, I felt safe, and more than fortunate to have rented the cute place in early 1974. An elderly couple, Mr. and Mrs. Campbell, owned the apartment which was situated above their garage. They kept their two cars in the garage, and I parked alongside the curb in front of the house. Their lovely two-story stone residence sat a few yards from the garage. The night of the warehouse fire, the Campbell's were out of town, visiting with their daughter and grandchildren for the weekend. They left one lamp on in the living room downstairs, which cast a soft light on the walkway that separated the garage from the back entrance to their house.

Suddenly aware that the once large crowd had thinned out, I quickly began the one block walk to my front door. At the same time, I became aware that I was being closely followed. I picked up the pace and made my way toward a parked fire truck across the street from my apartment—its lights were on. Unfortunately, I soon discovered that the truck was unmanned. Panic set in as I realized that the distance between the fast-approaching man and me was rapidly closing.

Unexpectedly, a kind-faced gentleman emerged from the alley next to my apartment to chat for a few minutes about the fire that was still smoldering a short distance away. I watched with anxious interest, as the man who had been following me, passed by without making eye contact. He headed to the end of the street and disappeared around the corner. Intent on getting back to the safety of my apartment, I wrapped up the very timely intervention with the kind gentleman and excused myself to walk to my front door. He said goodnight and then vanished.

I had no sooner retrieved my keys from my pocket, than the stalker appeared once again at the end of the street—now brazenly making his way toward me. I knew I didn't have the time needed to insert my key into the lock, open the door, and re-lock from the inside, so I made the instantaneous decision to run along the side walkway and through the door of the garage. Once inside, I could hear heavy footsteps approaching. As quiet as possible, I slid under Mr. Campbell's car, which was furthest from the door. With every breath, I prayed that the man would not look under the cars. I could see his shoes and hear him walking back and forth in the garage. After what seemed like an eternity, he finally left. Shaking uncontrollably, I remained under Mr. Campbell's car until daybreak—too afraid of the sinister shadows by night.

Serial killer, Ted Bundy, was in Boise on September 2, 1974. He later confessed before his execution on January 24, 1989, that he had raped and strangled a young woman on the outskirts of Boise, Idaho. He returned the next day to photograph and dismember her body before disposing of the remains in the Snake River.

My intuitive mother always believed my stalker that fateful night in early September 1974, was none other than the infamous Ted Bundy—and the timely intervention with a kind-faced gentleman was my blessed guardian angel. Nothing ever convinced her otherwise.

Christmas Came Early

She arrived in dramatic fashion,
cherished gift extraordinaire.

It seemed only fitting that our firstborn daughter would make her entrance in dramatic fashion—debuting on a cold December morning, just days before Christmas, as if she herself were the season's most extraordinary gift. Cindy's arrival was more than a joyous event; it was a turning point, a new chapter in our lives.

From the very beginning, Cindy was a child of adventure. For the first two years of her life, she traveled untold miles, her days and nights shaped by the rhythm of gospel music, the hum of diesel engines, and the ever-changing scenery outside the windows of our touring bus. She was cradled not only in *our* arms, but in the embrace of a community—musicians, friends, and a rotating cast of "on the road again" nannies who were delighted with her infectious laughter and boundless curiosity. Cindy quickly became the darling of the gospel music scene in the 1970s, her sparkling personality and easy adaptability winning hearts wherever she went.

Life on the road was a whirlwind of concerts, rehearsals, and late-night drives, but Cindy took it all in stride. She thrived in the spotlight, her expressive eyes and playful grin captivating audiences and fellow travelers alike.

One evening, when Cindy was just two years old, her dad asked the question that would become a cherished family story. "Cindy, tell me about God," he prompted, expecting a child's simple answer. She paused, brow furrowing in thoughtful contemplation, and then replied with innocent candor, "I don't think I know her." The words, so earnest and unfiltered, caught us off guard and made us laugh, but they also gave us pause. In that moment, we realized that our fast-paced, unconventional lifestyle—filled with music and movement—might be missing something essential: the quiet, steady tempo of home, the gentle lessons learned in the comfort of family routines.

It was then that we made a life-changing decision. We traded the Greyhound bus for a Buick, exchanged weekend travel for the peaceful predictability of life in the Pacific Northwest. The transition was not without its challenges, but we never regretted it.

In the years that followed, we discovered the beauty of slowing down, of savoring ordinary days and simple pleasures. Our family found a new harmony, not just in music, but in the way we experienced life.

Cherished Gift

Firstborn, first love,
A cherished gift, sent from above.
You fill our days with gentle light,
With kindness, warmth, and pure delight.
Thankful always, I remain—
For you, my child, my sweetest gain.
~ D. L. Norris

Life Unfolding

―⚬―

Embracing Hope and Facing Uncertainty

It was a season of profound transformation, filled with both hope and uncertainty. Ambitious dreams soared, even as some promises quietly faded away. Glancing back, I realize it was simply life unfolding—beautiful, unpredictable, and ever-changing.

Sunrises and Sunsets
Sunrises and sunsets, too many to recall.
Days are becoming shorter, the children not so small.
Where have all the years gone?
Is the oft repeated phrase.
What seemed like only moments ago,
Became ten thousand days.
D. L. Norris

Decade of Decadence

The 1980s: Of Change, Hope and a Little bit of Glitter.

The 1980s are often remembered as "the decade of decadence," but the era was far more than just a celebration of surplus. It was a time defined by pivotal events that continue to shape our world today. The Soviet Union began its dramatic collapse, AIDS emerged as a devastating global epidemic, and the groundwork was laid for a technological revolution with the birth of the Internet. Personally, the times were marked by change, hope, and a little bit of glitter.

Mount Saint Helens

The catastrophic eruption of Mount Saint Helens was preceded by a series of small earthquakes and steam-venting episodes that began in March 1980. These early warning signs gradually intensified, setting the stage for one of the most dramatic volcanic events in North American history. On the morning of May 18, at precisely 8:32 a.m. PDT, the mountain unleashed a massive explosive eruption. The force of the blast was extraordinary, with a volcanic explosivity index of 5, ranking it among the most powerful eruptions ever recorded on the continent.

The eruption radically reshaped the landscape, sending ash clouds high into the atmosphere and triggering landslides, mudflows, and widespread devastation. Communities across the Pacific Northwest felt the impact, as ash rained down for hundreds of miles, disrupting daily life and leaving a lasting mark on the region. The Mount Saint Helens eruption remains a vivid reminder of nature's unpredictable power and the resilience required to recover from such a monumental event.

At the time, we lived a mere 90 miles from Mount Saint Helens, and witnessed firsthand the ominous, dark skies and subsequent rain of gray ash that followed the massive eruption. Staring out her bedroom window, my three-year-old daughter exclaimed, "Look, Mommy, it's snowing."

Ronald Reagan

Republican Ronald Reagan was inaugurated as the 40th president of the United States on January 20, 1981, ushering in a new era of leadership and optimism. His presidency is perhaps best remembered for his powerful challenge to Soviet leader Mikhail Gorbachev: "Mr. Gorbachev, tear down this wall." These famous words, spoken in Berlin, became a defining moment in history. A few years later, I witnessed firsthand the impact of Reagan's legendary challenge.

ROYAL WEDDING

Prince Charles, heir to the British throne, entered a historic union with Lady Diana Spencer, captivating the attention of millions around the world. Their wedding, on July 29, 1981, was not only a grand royal event, but also a cultural milestone that transformed Lady Diana into one of the most beloved and iconic figures of her era. The ceremony, watched by a global audience, marked the beginning of a new chapter for the British monarchy and left an enduring impression on the hearts of people everywhere. Even my five-year-old daughter was mesmerized, exclaiming, "Oh, wow, Diana looks just like Cinderella!"

INTERNET

The Internet, a revolutionary electronic network designed to facilitate communication and information exchange among scientists, officially opened its virtual doors to the world on January 1, 1983. What began as a specialized tool for research collaboration quickly evolved into a global phenomenon, transforming nearly every aspect of modern life.

Vice President Al Gore famously remarked that the Internet would become the gateway to changing the world—and history has proven him right. Today, the Internet connects billions of people, empowers innovation, and serves as the backbone of our digital society, reshaping how we learn, work, and interact across the globe.

A sad admission, but all I know is that when the Internet is down, my world ceases to function efficiently.

Challenger Disaster

On the morning of January 28, 1986, the world watched in stunned disbelief as the United States space shuttle Challenger tragically exploded just 73 seconds after liftoff, instantly claiming the lives of all seven astronauts aboard. The crew included Francis R. Scobee, Michael J. Smith, Ronald McNair, Ellison Onizuka, Judith Resnik, Gregory Jarvis, and Christa McAuliffe—a high school teacher who had been selected to be the first civilian and educator in space, making the mission especially poignant for millions of students and teachers across the country.

The disaster unfolded live on television, with countless families, classrooms, and NASA personnel witnessing the catastrophic breakup of the shuttle against a clear blue sky. The loss was not only a devastating blow to the families of the crew, but also to the nation's spirit and the global scientific community. In the aftermath, investigations revealed that a faulty O-ring seal in the right solid rocket booster had failed due to the unusually cold temperatures that morning, allowing hot gases to escape and ultimately causing the shuttle's destruction. I remember that Tuesday morning vividly, as we watched the Challenger explosion—utterly horrified, we were. The image of Christa McAuliffe's parents and sister witnessing the tragedy will always be imprinted in my mind.

BERLIN WALL

For nearly three decades, the Berlin Wall stood as a stark and ominous symbol of the Cold War, encircling West Berlin and severing it from East Germany. Its concrete expanse, topped with barbed wire and guarded by watchtowers, represented not only a physical barrier but also the deep ideological divide between East and West. When the Wall finally fell on November 9, 1989, it marked a moment of profound transformation—freedom triumphed over oppression, and hope surged through a city long separated by fear and uncertainty.

In June of 1990, we had the unforgettable opportunity to visit the beautiful city of Berlin. Walking through its vibrant streets, we were drawn to the massive, graffitied remains of the Wall. Standing before this historic monument, I reached down and picked up a small piece of concrete to tuck into my bag—a humble fragment that, for me, became a poignant symbol of resilience and the enduring human spirit.

Far East Princess

Love knows no borders—one of our family's greatest gifts arrived from the far east.

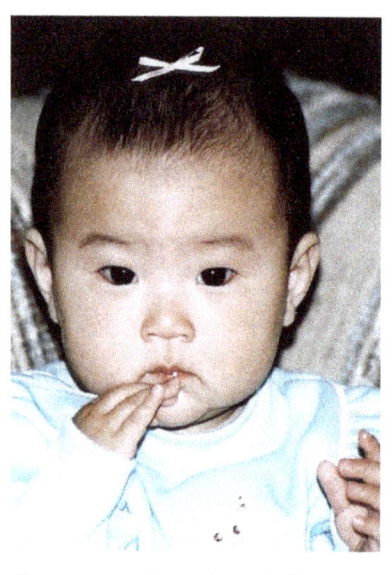

The 1980s were not only a time of global change and cultural transformation, but for our family, they became a decade marked by extraordinary joy and the blossoming of new beginnings. In the midst of the world's turbulence, we experienced a miracle of our own—the arrival of our beloved daughter, Lauren Elisabeth, from Seoul, Korea, on a crisp winter afternoon, January 7, 1986.

Her journey to us was the culmination of a year-long adoption process, filled with anticipation, paperwork, and countless prayers. Each step brought us closer to the moment we would finally meet her. I still remember the day our social worker, Colleen Mayberry, called with the news that a five-month-old baby girl was waiting for us. The excitement in our home was palpable; we could hardly contain our joy as we prepared to travel the 425 miles from Boise to Portland International Airport.

Lauren's arrival was unforgettable. After a thirteen-hour flight from Seoul, she was wide-eyed and alert, taking in her new surroundings with quiet curiosity. That first night, sleep eluded her—she gazed at us for hours, her dark eyes searching our faces as if trying to unravel the story of who we were and what her place might be in our family. It was as though she was deciding whether to trust us with her heart. Only after a long, silent vigil did she finally surrender to exhaustion, letting out a deep sigh and drifting into peaceful sleep. I guess we passed the test.

As the years unfolded, we watched Lauren grow and flourish, her spirit and personality blossoming just as her grandmother had so eloquently predicted. She became the beautiful rose in our family garden—resilient, vibrant, and full of life.

She has taught us about love that transcends borders and the true meaning of family. Through her, we have learned that bonds of the heart are just as strong—if not stronger—than those of blood. Her story is woven into the very fabric of our family, a testament to hope, perseverance, and the enduring power of love.

Sweet Child of My Own

Though not flesh of my flesh, or bone of my bone
You were born in my heart, sweet child of my own.
Before my arms held you, I knew, don't you see.
God had already planned that you belonged to me.
~ D. L. Norris

Dawn of a New Day

Revaluation and Redirection

The final decade of the twentieth century unfolded as an era of profound transformation. The rise of Google and Amazon accelerated the Internet's influence, reshaping daily life and connecting the world in ways previously unimaginable. On the global stage, the Cold War's long shadow finally lifted with the collapse of the Soviet Union, ushering in a new era of hope and uncertainty. Amid these sweeping changes, I sensed a stirring deep within—a quiet restlessness, an urge to reflect and redefine my own path. The world was shifting, and so was I. Was a new chapter about to begin?

Dawn of a New Day
In the silence before the morning breaks,
Dark shadows speak of past mistakes.
The world transforms, and hearts must too,
Paths once familiar now shift from view.
In dawn's gentle light, I find my way—
Guided by hope of a brighter day.
~ D. L. Norris

See You Later, Kid

*We sealed the deal with a prayer—
and then never again discussed our eternity pact.*

She left too soon. Yet, even knowing that, I could never be so selfish as to wish her back. I despise the cancer that took her away, but she is free now—her spirit is no longer captive in a body ravaged by pain. She is at peace, and with God.

I met Deb in the summer of 1964, just before we started ninth grade. She was instantly likable, with her bright smile and pixie-like features. I knew from the start that our friendship would last.

High school was brighter because of Deb. We shared lunches, chatted between classes, and even took a wild ride on the janitor's commercial vacuum cleaner—a misadventure for which we paid dearly. Our long, pleasant bus rides to and from school became cherished rituals. She brought so much joy to my life.

During our junior year, things changed. We traded bus rides for Chevy Corvairs—Deb's was black with a yellow interior, affectionately called the "Grand

Bumblebee," and mine was blue. They weren't new, but we didn't care. Taking turns behind the wheel, we often wondered how life could possibly get better.

One night, on a whim, we drove to a nearby town to try the French fries at a fast-food joint that claimed to have the best this side of the Mississippi. As we munched on our greasy snack, our conversation was light and irreverent—ranging from our opinions of librarian Mrs. Roberts and her sagging bustline to our disgust with Ronnie Lynd's disregard for personal hygiene. Then, without warning, our talk turned serious: heaven, and what happens when you die. Neither of us was ready to take flight, but the motive was clear—there was simply no way we could imagine being apart. So, in the glow of the parking lot lights, we bowed our heads in a solemn prayer, believing it would seal our destiny. With a sigh of relief, we set out for home, never again discussing our "eternity pact." Still, we both knew something significant had happened that night.

Deb has now gone to the heaven we spoke of so many years ago. I still struggle to believe she's gone. Time may ease the pain, but the sense of loss remains. I often wonder why our paths crossed, why our friendship endured thirty years of life's changes. The answer isn't simple. We had different dreams, any of which could have sent us in separate directions. But it never happened. Ours was a unique friendship—one that was certain, destined to continue beyond this life.

Just before she left, I held her hand and told her I loved her. She whispered the same. No further words were needed, because her eyes said the rest. There were no goodbyes; we had taken care of those years before. She just smiled and whispered, "See you later, kid."

Never Forget

My God, how could such an atrocity have taken place? More importantly, could it happen again?

Who was the little girl with blonde curls and unsuspecting eyes staring back at me? She could have easily been my own, anxiously waiting in line for one more ride on the carousel. But not *this* child. Instead, she quietly stood and waited her turn in a different sort of line. It appeared that she held something in her small hands, perhaps a favorite toy. Moments after this haunting photograph was taken, the little girl was ushered quickly, along with hundreds of others that day, into the gas chambers at Auschwitz.

Not even the soft-spoken words of Reverend Suski, "This will be a very hard day for you, so I will pray," could have adequately prepared me for that afternoon in June 1990.

We traveled by car to southern Poland with good friend Boguslaw, arriving at our destination a short time later. We approached the entrance of this ominous-looking place on foot. Miles of barbed wire fencing and towering lookouts betrayed the message on the huge iron gates—Arbeit Macht Frei (Work Makes Freedom). Absolutely nothing here spoke of freedom.

This was Auschwitz, the largest and most infamous of Nazi concentration and death camps. It was here that prisoners died from lethal injections, torture, starvation, slave labor, and lack of basic sanitary conditions. Many were the victims of criminal "medical" experiments at the evil hands of Dr. Josef Mengele. In all human history, there has never been a tragedy that has inspired such extensive reflection upon the morality of humankind such as the carnage that occurred at Auschwitz.

Standing at the entrance gates, I wondered what the millions of innocent victims must have felt as they moved through these same gates. Fear, powerlessness, a spark of hope?

The first groups of arriving prisoners were assured that Auschwitz was a work camp. They carried in sewing machines and tools, with the sincere hope that they could work hard in exchange for their eventual freedom. No one bothered to tell them that the average stay was less than thirty days. In time, the camp "welcome committee" would simply point to the crematorium and coldly inform new arrivals, "The only way you will leave Auschwitz is through the chimney."

We walked about the camp in solemn silence, too numb to show emotion. Others wept openly. Perhaps they had lost family members in this horrible place. A sickening feeling swept over me. Then anger. How could this atrocity have taken place?

The huge brick building which we entered next appeared to be a non-threatening structure at first. We were guided into rooms that contained personal items belonging to the prisoners; clothes, shoes, eyeglasses, hair ribbons, books, suitcases, and children's toys. However, we soon discovered that housed in this building were details of crimes unprecedented in history. What we learned, many have tried desperately to forget or pretend it did not happen. I will *never* forget. The pleading eyes of the little girl in the photograph will not allow me to do anything but remember.

We were led into cold, damp cells that had once been "home" to many a victim. We saw the small bunks which had once been lined with tick-infested straw, sleeping two or three prisoners per bed. Concrete structures centered in the barracks served as toilet facilities. I couldn't help but think of the degradation, the humiliation. These were human beings!

Entering one of the crematoriums where huge black ovens lined the brick walls, I tried in vain to disguise my shock when our guide stated that hundreds of prisoners were executed and cremated daily. The combined burning capacities of the five operating crematoriums at Auschwitz were 4,756 bodies in a 24-hour time period!

We walked slowly down the dirt path which led us back to the entrance gates once again, overcome with disbelief, yet unable to deny what we had heard and witnessed. I bent down and picked up two small rocks, placing them in my coat pocket. I wanted tangible evidence that this indeed was a place, and not just a frightening dream from which I would gratefully awaken.

Then suddenly I saw them. Hundreds of brightly colored flowers—tulips, daffodils, daisies—bloomed near one of the brick buildings which contained the gruesome details of an event in our history that some would prefer to eradicate from memory. Many cannot speak of it, as if silence will erase. Yet, those beautiful flowers which seemed so terribly out of place were anything but silent. They nearly shouted, "Life is precious, never forget."

> ...the righteous shall be in everlasting remembrance.
> Psalms 112:6

Keeper of Memories

*One brick at a time,
the keeper of my childhood memories was dismantled.*

I took a peaceful stroll through my old neighborhood this afternoon and started to pass by my childhood home for what I thought would be a happy walk down memory lane. I was heartbroken to see that a construction team was busy tearing down walls and rearranging the lot. My look of dismay obviously didn't go unnoticed, and one of the workers asked if I was all right. *All right?* Are you serious? You're dismantling a part of my childhood. How can I be all right? I knew that he couldn't possibly understand what this house meant to me with all the precious memories still deep within its crumbling walls. I stood for a long while, watching and remembering.

I was nine years old when we moved to Boise, Idaho, from Vallejo, California, in the spring of 1960. The trailer we pulled behind us was loaded to the hilt with furniture and other belongings. It was truly a sight to behold. The car was packed just as tightly with barely enough room for me, Mom, Dad, a golden Labrador puppy, and a bright yellow parakeet in a blue cage. The trek was long, and I wondered at times if we would ever make it to Boise. But, when we finally arrived, I immediately fell in love with the quaint little house in the east end of town. It was only 650 square feet, but it seemed like a mansion to me. Our street had more trees than I had ever seen in my life. Best of all, squirrels were everywhere!

After one week of settling into our new environment, I resumed third grade at Roosevelt Elementary, which was just two blocks from our house. Several days a week, I visited the Roosevelt Market that was situated directly across the street from the school grounds, leaning on the glass-front counter and selecting my favorite penny candy.

As I stared at the piles of rubble, a flood of precious memories washed over me—vivid images of my sweet mother came to mind. I remembered how eagerly she awaited news of my day at school, her always cheerful smile and infectious laughter, and her endless enthusiasm for helping me plan backyard carnivals for the neighborhood children. She was always willing to bake pink-frosted cupcakes so I could sell them for extra spending money, and she never hesitated to comfort me in the night when I was scared or feeling sick.

Equally strong were the soothing memories of my dad. I loved coming home from school to find him in his upholstery shop—the warm sound of the old brown RCA Radiola playing in the background, the steady hum of his sewing machine, and the familiar scent of wood varnish and paint thinner filling the air. Each evening, as I drifted off to sleep, my final recollection was always the same: hearing my dad wind the old cuckoo clock and double-check the front door lock, a simple ritual that made me feel safe and deeply loved.

There was so much happiness in that little house: visits from family and friends, birthday and holiday celebrations, sleepovers, and backyard picnics. It was also where I first experienced the death of someone dear to me.

I loved my Grandpa Gunderson, and my memories of him are rich. I remember the morning that my bedroom door opened slowly, and Mom told me that Grandpa had passed away during the night. He was eighty-one. I was thirteen. Through the years, I missed him deeply.

Ah, memories. Though I'll never see the quaint yellow house again, I know the treasures of my childhood remain alive and well within my heart. For that, I am deeply grateful—to have called such a delightful place my home, sweet home.

A Change of Season

Rediscovery and Resilience

Heart wrenching goodbyes are not for the faint of heart; the end of a thirty-year marriage, death of dear friends, and saying goodbye to my precious parents. All life-changing losses—but there were also unexpected blessings along the way. The rediscovery of a precious friendship following a painful divorce ensured that not all had been lost. A new love, a new life ushered in blessed redemption. Sweet memories faithfully followed death's anguish. Joyous life after loss is more than possible. Of this, I know.

In December
*God gives us memories,
So that we might have roses
in December.*
~ D. L. Norris

Second Chances

*No fanfare, or drama—
just the gentle unfolding of a new chapter.*

My second chance at love arrived not with a grand gesture or dramatic flourish, but with the gentle unfolding of a new chapter—quiet, steady, and full of grace. There was no soundtrack, no "our song" to mark the moment; instead, it was the soft dawn of possibility, the comforting warmth of a heart opening again after loss. Quincy entered my life with kindness as his calling card, a man whose goodness radiated in small, everyday actions.

From the beginning, I sensed that Quincy's love was genuine, rooted not only in affection for me but in a profound compassion for those I held dear. When he said, "I do," he pledged himself not just to me, but to the family I cherished—especially my aging parents, whose needs had grown with the passing years. For this, I am forever grateful. His devotion to them was unwavering, his patience inexhaustible. In moments when uncertainty clouded their days, Quincy was a beacon of reassurance. "You don't ever have to worry. I'll always take care of you," he promised, and his words were more than comfort—they were a lifeline.

He became their steady presence, tending to their worries with gentle words and soothing their fears with a compassionate touch. Whether it was a reassuring hand on my dad's shoulder or a quiet conversation with my mother in the late afternoon, Quincy's care was both practical and deeply heartfelt. He never hesitated, never faltered, even when the responsibilities of caregiving grew heavy. In the darkest hours, when my parents looked for hope, Quincy was there—offering not just help, but dignity and respect.

I have come to love him in ways I never expected, not only for the tenderness he shows me, but for the boundless kindness he extends to those I love the most. There is a special kind of gratitude reserved for those who love your family as their own, who step into the role of caretaker with humility and grace. Quincy's devotion has woven itself into the fabric of our lives, a quiet testament to the power of second chances and the healing that love can bring.

Dawn After Night
Love returns softly,
like dawn after night—
a heart once broken
finds new light.
~ D. L. Norris

Finishing Well

Nothing mattered more than guiding them with love and dignity as they made their final journey from this world to the next.

The mission was clear—there was nothing quite so important as helping my beloved parents transition gracefully from this world to the next. In that moment, all ambitions for book-writing, editing, and marketing faded into the background, eclipsed by a calling that felt sacred and urgent. Life has a way of rearranging priorities, and when this divine intervention arrived, it demanded our full attention and devotion. We both agreed, this was a higher calling, one that required me to set aside personal pursuits and dedicate myself wholly to the care of my sweet, aging parents. With the unwavering support of my husband, Quincy, whose compassion and steadiness became my anchor, we both embraced the commission to help them finish well.

The early days of caregiving were bright and filled with heartwarming scenes; Dad and Quincy playing the ukulele and singing old hymns; Mom and I reminiscing about old times and laughing until we cried; going to church as a family, and having brunch afterward at our favorite restaurant; Mom mistakenly wearing Dad's black pants, and the round of laughter that ensued once it was discovered. They were simply delightful times!

As we expected, within a short time, their physical and mental decline became more apparent and required a different level of care. Still, they were so appreciative of our presence and never failed to express their gratitude. I kept Mom's nails trimmed and polished in her favorite color. Quincy saw to it that Dad was always well-shaven. There was joy in knowing that they were well cared for—and happy.

The journey that followed—spanning more than two years—was a beautiful tapestry of challenge and blessing. There were days marked by fatigue, worry, and the inevitable frustration that accompanies the role of caregiver. Yet, these moments were consistently overshadowed by a heavenly bounty of grace, mercy, and love that seemed to multiply with each passing day.

I cherished the quiet hours spent holding my mother's hand, listening to her stories, and offering comfort during anxious days. I found joy in preparing my dad's favorite meals, in the familiar sound of his voice, and in the peaceful assurance that he was safe and loved. Each day became a gift, an opportunity to honor the legacy of two remarkable lives and to express gratitude for the countless sacrifices they had made for our family through the years.

Looking back, I can say with certainty that I will never regret a single moment caring for my precious parents. The experience transformed me, deepened my capacity for empathy, and taught me the true meaning of devotion. To help them finish well was not only an act of love, but it was also a profound blessing, one that will remain engraved on my heart forever.

Imaginary Horse

Dementia is no laughing matter, but threatening to ride off on a horse brought much-needed smiles.

They were heartbreaking days. My dad couldn't accept the fact that he had entered the sunset season of his life—a place where it was no longer safe for him to drive. He was 91.

"You don't understand," he said, angrily, smacking the newspaper on the mahogany side table next to his recliner. *There* he was, the strong-willed Norwegian had entered the room. "I've been driving since I was fourteen years old!" This time, I felt his deep pain. His lip trembled, and my heart broke.

It was imperative that I do this right, I reminded myself—not just for him, but for me, as well. Undoubtedly, I, too, would walk the same road in a few years. "Papa, I'll take you anywhere you want to go," I assured, taking his hand, while holding back my *own* tears. Being empathetic had to be balanced with gently convincing him that it was time to relinquish the keys. A few close calls of running stop signs, taking wrong turns, and getting lost several miles from home were all catalysts for re-evaluating where we were as a family. The signs of dementia were evident, and I worried about him—*and* Mom, as his faithful, though often frightened, passenger.

I held his hand and shed tears along with him. "I understand, Papa, and I love you." After a few moments of shared emotion, he squared his shoulders and proclaimed, "Well, I may not be able to drive a car, but there's no law that says I can't ride a horse." I smiled and breathed a sigh of relief. Papa always had the last word, and this time, he had earned it.

When I Leave

I should have known that she would depart on her own terms— and did she ever!

It was a conversation that I was not comfortable with, purely for selfish reasons. I simply was not ready to let my mama go. For over sixty-five years she had beautifully and consistently influenced my life with her sweet, loving ways. To carry on without her was beyond my comprehension. But she insisted that we discuss how she viewed her imminent departure from this world. I had no choice but to listen. I fought back the tears that threatened to spill over. A sob was forming in the deep recesses of my soul. She spoke with certainty and confidence that belied any anxiety she may have been experiencing at the moment. "I need to know that you'll be okay when I leave." She paused for a moment as if to gather her thoughts. "I think it will be hard for you because we have been so close." She smiled while remembering all the wonderful times we had shared together. "Hasn't our relationship just been the sweetest?" I nodded in agreement, although I was still struggling for composure. She glanced out the kitchen window and took a deep breath. "I've been seeing loved ones that are in heaven." She looked at me for a long moment, studying my expression, before adding, "Especially my grandma." I swallowed hard because I believed her. She loved her grandma and had told me so many precious stories about her through the years. They were close, too, and it made sense that her grandma would be anxious to see her. No doubt, my mama was being prepared to transition from this life to the next, and my heart knew that she wouldn't be with us for long. "You know where I'll be, don't you?" she asked. Of course, I did. I just didn't want her to leave.

On October 10, 2017, she took a serious fall that fractured her back in three places. Her doctor was swift to inform us that she would not be returning home any time soon and that the road to recovery—if there was to be a recovery at all—was a long, arduous journey considering her 90 years of age. Ultimately, she decided that the battle was not one she had the strength to wage. In eleven days, her earthly struggle came to an end. I knew she was with the Lord, but my heart was beyond broken.

I've not talked much about the last day she spent on earth and reasoned that her passing was such a personal matter that I need not share the details. As time goes by, I've had a change of heart. There were some remarkable, God-filled moments during the several hours leading up to my mama's transition and ultimate departure that I feel compelled to share.

On the morning of October 21, 2017, Mama was in a deep coma, and we knew that her death was forthcoming. Nurses adjusted levels of pain medication as they deemed necessary for her to remain comfortable and free of distress. They regularly swabbed her mouth with ice water and placed pillows under and around her back for support. Shortly after 2:30 pm, my sister and I were talking in the doorway of her room. Suddenly, we were both aware of a presence that rushed past us. Our knees buckled simultaneously, and we reached for each other so as not to lose our balance. My sister exclaimed, "Oh my goodness, Deb, they're here." We knew instinctively that heavenly angels filled the room. The nurse that was attending her looked alarmed, asking, "What just happened?" She quickly checked for a pulse and could not locate one. Her breathing stopped for what we believed was the last time. I glanced at the room clock to see that it was almost 2:40 pm. Suddenly, she gasped for air, and her pulse was again detectable. I felt a deep sense of relief mixed with immense confusion as to what had just occurred. The presence that so engulfed the room shortly before was now gone. For the next seven hours, her breathing was labored but steady. At 10:05 pm, her very tired body stopped struggling.

The next two weeks were dark and full of questions, most of which I dared not express. Why had Mama stayed so long after angels had come to escort her home? Were we mistaken? Had she suffered? The grief and the questions which tortured my soul were nearly unbearable.

When the death certificates finally arrived at the funeral home, I was called to come to the office and review them for accuracy. To my utter amazement, the time of death that was recorded and certified by the doctor was 2:39 pm! No one will ever persuade me otherwise that my mama left with the holy angels. There are just some things we cannot explain on this side of heaven, and it's best not to try.

Over the Rainbow
Somewhere over the rainbow,
You are tending beautiful blooms.
Roses, tulips and daffodils,
many others, I presume.
Heavenly flowers all cared for by you,
Nurtured by His sunlight
and blessed morning dew.
In your garden so lovely,
no pests or thorns to hurt.
You are always young and beautiful,
in Levi's and a crisp white shirt.
~ D. L. Norris

Bearing One Another's Burdens

*The "firsts" were nearly unbearable—
then, an unexpected blessing arrived.*

There were days after my precious mother passed away that it was difficult to breathe. The "firsts" caught me off guard; Thanksgiving, Christmas, my birthday (and the traditional "Mama Cake"), New Year's, and the cold, gray trip to the cemetery for the first time where I wept uncontrollably. Not far from me stood a white-haired, elderly man, stooped over a granite grave marker who was doing the same. My heart hurt more so for him, as he steadied himself with a cane. Perhaps he reminded me of my sweet dad who, at the time, was a resident at a nearby memory care facility, no longer able to live alone or with us because of the level of care required for advanced dementia. The sad difference was that the elderly man at the cemetery was grieving deeply—my precious dad no longer remembered my mother, his wife of seventy-two years. The combined loss of both parents, though different in nature, was immense.

I remember the day vividly as I left the house for a dental procedure that would no longer tolerate my procrastination. Three hours later, I stood up with numbness from my nose to my chin. The dentist congratulated me for being such a good patient and putting up with a long, complicated procedure. He didn't even chastise me for procrastination. I suspect he knew I had suffered sufficiently. He smiled and left the room.

I put on my coat and picked up my purse. Out of the blue, the dental assistant shared with me that her father's death was imminent and that she didn't know how she would eventually deal with the loss and grief. The moments that followed felt surreal. I saw my hand reach for hers—and then heard the sound of my voice, "Honey, some days you'll feel like you can't breathe. The pain of loss will be great. Grief is the price we pay for loving someone with all of our heart." She cried and reached out for comfort. "I know how you feel right now," I assured her. "But, trust me, in time you will smile again." Listen to me, talking as if I were a grief counselor. There I was, comforting a hurting soul who was grieving someone still living. But, grieving, nonetheless. I told her that I would remember to pray for her and her family. Strangely, I turned and walked out the door with a lightness in my step that had long been absent.

I can't help but recall a familiar Scripture that speaks of 'bearing one another's burdens.' Isn't that precisely what lightens our own?

Ageless Beauty

She left with the angels, but her beauty dances in every memory.

She is a picture of ageless beauty, the kind that doesn't lose sleep over wrinkles. It emanates from deep within—the sweet essence of the soul. I imagine that many will not be fortunate enough to experience this for themselves, perhaps not even know of someone who possesses this unique beauty. I was blessed beyond measure to know her—she was my mother. I'd say she is no longer with us, but that would not be entirely true. She left with the angels on a colorful autumn day, but her legacy lives on in the hearts of her family. In that respect, she is still very *much* with us.

She prayed incessantly for family members and for anyone else that "God placed on my heart" as she would say. Those prayers are still accomplishing their work. She loved babies and children, whether they were her own or someone else's. She didn't tolerate unruly behavior when little ones came to visit but was a true master of distraction; cookies, juice, and stories always seemed to do the trick. She kept countless journals, diaries, and notes as she always explained, "to keep track of my many blessings."

She laughed heartily; in fact, many of my favorite photos and memories of her are those with a full, open mouth expression of delight. She brought joy, love, and a cake to nearly every gathering. When her eyesight deteriorated because of macular degeneration and glaucoma, I found it challenging to keep the tears back. She loved sewing, crocheting, reading, and cooking—and would eventually lose the ability to enjoy most of these pastimes. But, instead of lamenting this new reality, she would say with a smile, "I've seen a multitude of beautiful things, and they are all in my memory bank for safekeeping."

Ageless beauty, grace, and wisdom. She lived ninety beautiful years and was a blessing to all who were privileged to know and love her.

The Garden of Memory
Her essence lingers in the air,
A gentle smile, a loving prayer.
Life, it fades, but grace remains—
Her spirit dances to love's refrain.
She gathered blessings, day by day,
With kindness that will always stay.
Though gone with angels, she lives on—
In the garden of memory, singing love's sweet song.
~ D. L. Norris

Touched By an Angel

It was because of Judy, that I had a welcome reprieve from my grief.

I dreaded the painful task ahead of me and had been procrastinating for far too long—today was the day that I would finally handle the business of changing my dad's primary death benefit recipient from my mother to his secondary heirs. *Why* was this so hard? It seemed that anything requiring the permanent removal of my mother's name, whether it be from a checking account or a credit card, had been grievous. To be honest, the thought of dealing with a customer service representative this morning was about as welcome as a root canal. The inevitable series of questions, not to mention the usual cold demeanor of the stranger on the other end of the telephone, was already setting me on the defense. A problematic chore was only more challenging when discussing a personal topic with someone who had no emotional investment. I dialed the number and readied myself for a voice that would likely grate on my deeply wounded heart.

I was not prepared for Judy. The voice was soft, but clear. Her question, "What can I do to help you, Deborah?" not only took me by surprise, but her tender tone made me feel vulnerable. I gave her the pertinent information needed to process my request, but once that was accomplished, and she informed me that everything was now in order, she began to speak as though she understood my very heart. "Deborah, tell me about your dad," she began. "How is he handling the loss of your mother?" When I told her that they had shared 72 years of marriage, she gasped. "Oh, how wonderful!" I proceeded to tell her about Dad's dementia and how he didn't remember my mother, nor recall much of anything regarding his family. Again, Judy responded with tender words that soothed my soul. "God has placed a gentle covering over his mind to protect him from the grief of your mother's passing." She continued with a caring tone, and I found myself wondering how she could speak so freely in a workplace environment. "Deborah, my mother passed away almost two years ago, and I miss her every day," she shared. "But here is what I want to tell you. Our mothers have simply changed addresses, having moved to their heavenly home. They both traded tired bodies for a glorious place where there is no pain." I gave into my grief. "Deborah, here is the best news. We *will* see them again."

After a precious twenty-minute conversation, Judy said how much she enjoyed visiting with me. Following a tearful goodbye, I couldn't help but wonder who I had been so privileged to visit with. *Really.*

A Life Well-Lived

If you were kind, then you had a seat at Mama's table.

Anyone who knows me, even casually, understands how much I love my mama. She was such a joy in my life, and it goes without saying that I miss her every day. Still, her legacy continues—in *my* heart and in the hearts of those who were influenced by her life. One thing that always made me so incredibly proud of her was how she conducted her life. She built a strong and unwavering foundation of love—extended to everyone regardless of faith, politics, lifestyle preference, or ethnicity. Clearly, if you were kind, then you had a seat at my mama's table. Plain and simple.

I remember on several occasions, going to visit her and Dad on a Saturday morning only to be warmly introduced to door-to-door missionaries sitting in the living room. Happily sipping coffee and enjoying my mama's freshly baked cinnamon rolls, they were not there to preach or convince her that she needed to convert to their beliefs. No, that had been established long before that they need not waste their time by attempting to sway her from her own solid faith. They were there because they were kind, and that was always enough for my mama to call them friends and serve them a cinnamon roll. In the beginning, she had gently reminded them when they were getting ready to depart, "Here, honey, you can take your brochure with you." This weekly visit based on mutual love and respect continued through the years and was simply a small gathering of precious ladies sharing life and relationship. My mama had such an array of friends—for at least one very delightful reason. She was never judgmental, and everyone was welcome.

Stories of her life, legacy, and Godly example are endless and could easily fill a book or two. Thank you, my sweet mama. You took a part of my heart when you went away, but you left me so much more. My life has your fingerprints all over it. Until we meet again.

Thief of Memories

A daughter's heartfelt tribute to her father, whose spirit endures even as dementia quietly steals his memories.

The gray corridor is long, and dimly lit. Empty bookshelves now line the walls where volumes of life history once resided; fascinating stories of childhood, colorful memories of travel, immense talent, endless expressions of love, and a great legacy of family. One by one, the books have silently been removed from the shelves and cast into an irretrievable space.

Dad was born on Monday, March 15, 1926, at a time in American history when Calvin Coolidge was the President of the United States, when you could purchase a new house for $7700 or rent one for $20 a month, buy a new car for $360, fill your gas tank for $.12 a gallon, and pick up a loaf of bread for $.09. A simpler time? Not according to stories told by my dad through the years. Life was difficult, and not for the faint of heart. He managed to live through the respective Dust Bowl and drought eras of the Midwest and later survive a near-fatal bout of Scarlet Fever and a kamikaze attack on his U.S. Navy ship *Goodhue* in the Asiatic Pacific. He eventually made his way back to the states to meet and marry my mother, a blessed union that would last for 72 years. My sister and I made him a wonderful, long-suffering, patient, and caring father. Seriously.

Dad. My hero, my safe place. My childhood memories of him are many, far too many to capture in this simple writing. I loved coming home from school and finding him in his upholstery shop— the old brown RCA Radiola playing in the background, the steady hum of a sewing machine, the smell of wood varnish and paint thinner, and the delightful discovery of leftover scraps of fabric on the shop floor that were destined to become articles of clothing for my dolls. At the close of each evening, my last recollections before drifting off to sleep were of hearing my dad winding the old cuckoo clock and rechecking the front door lock. My, how safe and secure I felt. I always knew where to find him, and there was little need to be anxious or afraid.

Now, in his twilight years, there is a quiet, notorious thief that creeps in and steals one precious memory at a time. I feel I may have lost sight of my dad for the first time, somewhere along the winding road of dementia. Strangely, he is content in his new world. He doesn't worry. He doesn't recall painful events or losses. He only lives in the here and now. A protective shell of no remembrance covers his mind. He is genuinely thankful for the small things; a comfortable chair, a warm blanket, a nourishing meal, simple conversation involving current events, a friendly voice, a gentle touch, and a handful of unsalted peanuts.

For all the countless memories that have been stolen, there remains something miraculously untouched by this ravaging disease—his spirit. I catch glimpses of his kindness, gentleness, and loving ways. I see the smile that lights up his face and eyes, all poignant reminders that he is in there somewhere. My heart knows it. Occasionally he will ask me, "Have I always lived here?" Oh my. I take a deep, emotion-filled breath. "No, my sweet Papa," I say, fighting back tears while taking his weathered hand in mine. "You have traveled the world, once upon a time. In your 94 years, you have experienced a myriad of wonders. Why, the many stories of your life could easily fill volumes."

On April 29, 2020, Papa took a final, peaceful breath, and faded quietly into the sunset. Oh, how we miss his sweet essence.

Ode to Papa

My life—a tapestry, woven by hands unseen.
I do not choose the colors,
or patterns that might have been.

Sometimes sorrow threads its way,
And pride clouds what I see,
Yet above, the pattern forms
Beyond my clarity.

Dark threads and golden strands,
Each needed in the plan
All woven by the Master's skill,
And by His guiding hand.
~ D. L. Norris

Thanks for the Memories

He was gone too soon—and for a moment time stood still.

The sudden death of their father was a shattering, life-altering event for my two daughters. Nothing could have prepared them for the abruptness of loss—the way ordinary days can be transformed in an instant, leaving behind a silence that echoes through every corner of the heart. At seventy-one, he was the very picture of health and vibrance, a steady presence whose laughter and wisdom filled their lives. And then, in a moment, everything changed. He was gone.

For me, his passing was not only a personal heartbreak, but a profound shift in the landscape of my own history. Even though I had remarried long before his death, the impact of losing someone who had been such a significant part of my life journey left a tremendous void. He was more than an ex-husband; he was a dear friend, a once upon a time companion through decades of shared memories, triumphs, and trials. The tapestry of our lives was woven together with threads of love, forgiveness, and mutual respect—bonds that endured even as our paths diverged.

I often find myself revisiting a particular scene from a few years ago, one that now glows in my memory with the gentle light of grace. Both Tom and Quincy were visiting in our backyard, their camaraderie and animated conversation filling the air. They were both hand-talkers, their gestures painting stories in the space between. Watching them together, I felt a profound sense of gratitude—a deep recognition of God's redeeming grace revealed in one tangible, heartwarming moment. It was as if the past and present had come together, not in conflict, but in harmony, reminding me that love and friendship can transcend the boundaries of time and circumstance.

Tom, we'll see you again—the promise of reunion softens the ache of separation for our daughters. Thank you for the laughter, the lessons, and the love that continues to shape our lives. Thank you for showing us that even in loss, there is room for hope, and that the bonds we forge in this life are never truly broken. Your legacy lives on in the hearts of those who loved you, and your memory is a blessing we will cherish always. Thanks for the memories.

The Stories They Told

―∞―

Memoirs of long ago give life to the shadows of the past.

Thank goodness the older generation of my family shared so many wonderful stories of long-ago ancestors. They introduced me to more than just dates and places of birth. I feel I know many of them personally, though there are hundreds of years that separate us. Being acquainted with the way they lived, how they loved, and what they believed has been a life-changing journey into their respective lives. How grateful I am to "know" them.

A Living Museum
Our memories are like a living museum.
In each of its galleries,
No matter how narrow or dimly lit
Preserved forever are moments
Of loving and being loved.
~ D. L. Norris

Tenderhearted Charmer

"Mama, don't worry, I'm not afraid to die."
They were his last words, and then he was gone.

As soon as they were old enough to stand on their own two feet, the Gunderson children were expected to do their share of household chores and endless tasks on the farm. Omer was by no means an exception to this rule. But the tenderhearted charmer was also a soft touch for nature's beauty and carefully nurtured a flower garden with many beautiful varieties. He built a fence around his cherished, colorful blooms to keep the pesky chickens out.

In the spring of 1924, a day that began like any other ended in overwhelming sorrow for the Gunderson family. While climbing over a fence to go rabbit hunting, an accidental blast from the shotgun of his cousin would take Omer's life.

He died tragically on May 29, 1924, at the age of twelve years old. Omer's last words to his mother were, "Mama, don't worry, I'm not afraid to die." Sophie, my grandmother, who was nine months pregnant with her sixth child, cradled her firstborn son in her arms as he quietly passed away.

Omer Conrad Gunderson was buried in the North Branch Cemetery in Boone County, Nebraska. Seventy-seven years following his death, a granite grave marker was placed at his burial site in honor of his brief, yet so very precious life. It was my utmost privilege to accompany my family to Nebraska in June 2001 and take part in this special event. I found it difficult to contain my emotions as I watched Omer's two brothers, Kenneth and Vern carry the marker to the gravesite to honor the life of their oldest brother.

On a distant, grassy hillside, the old Gunderson farmhouse could be seen, a silent reminder of the love, laughter and grief which had once upon a time dwelt within its walls.

Faded Dreams

―∾―

He waited for twelve years, but no one ever came.

Otto Emil Dyrebu was born on Monday, April 6, 1874, in Dane County, Wisconsin, the first child and only son of my great-grandparents Kittil and Marte Fønnerud Dyrebu. At the time, Ulysses S. Grant was the President, and the era was marked by Indian wars and grasshopper plagues.

Otto was a kind, gentle, and long-suffering man who loved his family above all else. I say that he was long-suffering because of a sweet recollection shared by my dad regarding how his uncle Otto once handed him a pair of scissors and a straight razor with instructions to give him a much-needed haircut. Nervous at first, Dad obediently performed the task and then routinely kept his uncle's hair trimmed thereafter— each time very happily for a nickel. One haircut led to many more, and by the time Dad had fairly well mastered the art of haircutting, Otto had endured more than his share of embarrassing trims at the amateur hands of his ten-year-old nephew. But, no matter what, Otto always had encouraging words. "Don't worry, you'll learn in time. Just keep trying." His words were not only affirming but prophetic. Many years later, Dad went on to ensure that his U.S. Navy buddies always looked quite smart, and as the ship's barber, he also made a handsome sum for his well-honed skill. He was quick to credit his uncle Otto as the one who gave him his start.

Otto was a remarkably accomplished horseman and avid reader. He possessed numerous horses and just as many old books by notable authors.

He was a stout man with steel blue eyes and blonde hair, favoring many of his Norwegian ancestors. Otto always slept facing the east, whether cultural or superstitious and consistently adhered to this ritual. He carried a compass with him so that when away from home, his bed could be aligned to accommodate his sleeping preferences. Otto was known for keeping a small stash of Limburger cheese and a piece of lefse in his shirt pocket.

For the better part of my life, what I've written is what I was told of of Otto Emil Dyrebu. I suppose it's the best of recollections because the stories of his life at this time conjure good memories of a thoughtful man whose love was surely reciprocated. However, it was not until 1995, forty-seven years after Otto's death, that my dad tearfully told me the truth of his last painful years.

The Dyrebu's were a close-knit family, where shared mealtimes and after-church gatherings were a regular occurrence. No one was prepared for the 1930s drought that devastated the economy and plunged the country into a debilitating depression. Despite their best efforts to save the farm, they were unsuccessful. The first family to leave Nebraska was Otto's oldest sister and her husband, whom he had lived with for many years. When Otto realized he would not be going with them, the thought of living in the old house alone was particularly frightening to him. He tried desperately to convince them to take him to Idaho, eventually offering to leave all his belongings to lighten the load. To no avail, they promised to come back for him as soon as possible. He never saw them again. The last family to leave was Otto's youngest sister, her husband, and their children in 1940. Again, he begged to go with them to California. The same promise was made—a return once they were settled. It would be in the spring of 1944 before a family member made the trip to Nebraska to visit him. Otto thought that someone had finally arrived to retrieve him after twelve years. Sadly, it would not be the case and marked the last time he saw any of his relatives.

It was a nearby neighbor who occasionally checked in on him who realized Otto's health was rapidly declining and that he should no longer live by himself. The dream of being reunited with his beloved family had all but faded from Otto's memory—taking a toll on his body and heart.

Otto Emil Dyrebu passed away, quietly and very much alone, at the age of seventy-four in a Newman Grove, Nebraska, nursing facility on Wednesday, February 4, 1948.

Sworn to Secrecy

Mystery was his inheritance—and ours to unravel.

For as long as I can remember, there was such mystery surrounding the life of my great-grandfather. It's precisely the way he wanted it. In fact, when his own wife asked him questions about his early life, he adamantly refused to discuss the matter. The taboo subject was reluctantly respected throughout the years, especially after he said, "For the curious, they can wait until I'm dead to start asking questions." Of course, the speculation as to who he *really* was paved the way for endless, colorful dialogue—everything from vagabond to royalty.

After extensive research, here's what I know (and partly assume) of the man known as Grandpa Lindley.

Lindley Murray, my great-grandfather was born on April 14, 1865 in Trinidad, British West Indies to unmarried seventeen-year-old Christina Goldie, daughter of the prestigious Daniel Goldie and Isabella Gilchrist of Kilmaurs, Ayrshire, Scotland. There were a number of Goldie's residing in Trinidad and Christina was sent to live with relatives until the birth of her baby. The story was told that she would eventually marry Lindley's father, James Frederick Murray of Edinburgh, Scotland, although there is no record of this union, nor is there proof that James was even the baby's father. Lindley's birth record states "father unknown."

Accompanied by his tutor, Peter Finche, to assure a proper education, Lindley left his family and his home in Trinidad at the age of eleven. His mother returned to her homeland of Scotland to begin a new life. When the young boy wasn't tending to his daily studies, he was intent on earning a modest sum of money as a cabin boy aboard ship. Between the years of 1876 and 1882, nothing is known of Lindley's whereabouts or his life, however, he *is* listed as a passenger on the ship "Cameo" arriving at the Port of New York on April 12, 1883.

In 1883, Lindley worked on the construction of several buildings for the upcoming 1893 World's Fair in Chicago, Illinois. He met and married Olga Crahe of Berlin, Germany on May 4, 1891, in Chicago, but after four years, their marriage dissolved. He remained in Chicago for the next five years and became deeply involved in the local political arena—particularly the Democratic party.

Lindley eventually married my great-grandmother, Mary Missouri Fry, on April 30, 1896, in Columbus, Kansas. His life from this point on became something entirely different than that of the former. It's possible that Lindley was ashamed of the fact that he was born to a young single woman (his mother and grandparents certainly reacted as such) and determined to live a life sworn to secrecy. He and Mary had had ten children, and the family lived in Cripple Creek, Colorado and Kildare, Oklahoma before moving to and homesteading in Prairie Grove, Arkansas.

Lindley had an artistic flair when it came to painting and wallpapering and often assisted friends and family members with home decorating projects. He was an excellent cook, owning and operating a café in Fayetteville, Arkansas for several years. Long-time patrons claimed he made some of the best biscuits in the world, though it's doubtful that many world travelers resided in Fayetteville at the time.

They say you can gain remarkable insight into a person's character by reading letters that they have composed. If there is indeed truth to this assertion, Lindley must have been a very gentle and compassionate man. The following passages are taken from two letters that he wrote to his oldest son, Andrew—my grandfather.

January 9, 1927

My dear Son,

I am just so proud to be able to write to you that I can hardly contain myself. I am out of ink, so I will try to finish with a pencil. Your last letter deserves an answer. I am so proud of my boy, and your letter will be a keepsake for the rest of my days. I wish I could come to Tulsa and stay for a month or so. I think perhaps the change would do some good. But I am afraid I would be too much trouble. If I had enough strength to walk around a little each day, I might gather some flesh and get stronger. My dear boy, you said that you think a lot of me and that you love me. It fills my heart with gladness to hear you say that, for I sure love you too and think of you all the time.

September 8, 1927

My dear Son,

I will write you a line to let you know that we are all right. I have not been feeling good lately. We are so proud of the baby, and you sure have given her the sweetest name. You and Lena must kiss her lots for me. Son, I do want to see you so bad even if for just a day or two. But I realize just the kind of fix you are in, so tied up with work. Now I believe I must close for the time. So, goodbye and good luck. A lot of kisses for the babies, and hugs for you and Lena.

Ten days after this last letter was written, Lindley Murray passed away quietly at his home in Fayetteville, Arkansas at the age of sixty-two following a four-year battle with cancer.

A Better Tomorrow

A dream set sail—and a new world awaited on the distant horizon.

She slipped quietly from her bed and dressed in the pre-dawn darkness, her fingers fumbling with the small buttons on the waistband of her blue, handmade skirt. Never before had she experienced such a myriad of emotions; excitement, fear, happiness, uncertainty. Today, her life would change forever.

In just a few hours, she and her uncle would begin their journey from Norway to America. They had talked about this supposed land of wealth and opportunity for months. She had dreamt about it even longer. A stirring in the kitchen area of the three-room cottage roused her from her deep thoughts. Obviously, she was not the only one awake at this early morning hour. She finished brushing her long blonde hair, and with a quick twist and a couple of hairpins, fastened it securely behind her head. Despite protests the night before about eating breakfast, her grandmother had insisted that she have a proper meal to start the day. There was no need to argue. For seventeen years, her grandmother's firm but loving hand had cared for her. This day would be no different. Reluctantly, she seated herself at the table and proceeded to pick at the food on her plate, all the while oblivious to the older woman's disapproving glances. When her grandmother turned to get a cup and saucer from the old corner cabinet, the girl placed the remaining bread and cheese in her skirt pocket. The small victory was bittersweet. Although there had been many a battle of wills throughout the years, she loved her strong and outspoken grandmother. For the most part, she was grateful for her guidance.

At last, the hour of departure had arrived. An old family trunk that had belonged to her deceased mother was quickly hoisted onto the back of the horse-drawn wagon. Two additional wooden boxes that held provisions sufficient to last until the journey's end were also placed in the back of the wagon. A hurried embrace and a weak smile were exchanged between the young girl and the old woman. Anything more would have been too painful.

Seated in the wagon next to her uncle, the two traveled in silence to a nearby dock where a boat would transport them to Bergen. Once they arrived in Bergen, they would board the great sailing vessel *Mercator* and join 400 other emigrants, all of which dreamt of a better tomorrow.

The young and determined seventeen-year-old would eventually arrive in Quebec, Canada. Her beloved uncle did not survive the harsh conditions of the journey and was buried in the frigid waters of the North Sea.

NOTE: *Ingeborg Nilsdtr Rutlin, my great-grandmother, left her birthplace of Sogndal, Norway, at the age of seventeen bound for America on the ship Mercator. Her uncle Berent and 72 other Sogndal residents accompanied her. Sadly, Ingeborg's twenty-nine-year-old uncle died of pneumonia in route, but the young Ingeborg arrived safely in Quebec, Canada, on June 30, 1870. From Quebec, she traveled by train, steamboat, and wagon to eventually reach her destination of Stoughton, Wisconsin.*

The Red Bean

―∽―

With a little creativity, she turned a bland meal into a magical treasure hunt.

Throughout the years, my mother delighted in sharing stories drawn from her vast treasury of cherished memories. Each tale she recounted was like a precious gem, illuminating the lives and personalities of family members, transforming names and dates into vivid, living portraits. I am profoundly grateful for these recollections, for they have created a beautiful, and deeply meaningful tapestry of family stories.

One story, in particular, stands out—a simple tradition that brought warmth and laughter to the Murray family's dinner table. Beans and cornbread might sound like a humble, even ordinary meal, but my grandmother possessed a remarkable gift for turning the mundane into something magical. Her secret was an ingenious twist: while preparing the pot of white beans, she would quietly slip a single red bean into the simmering mixture. The anticipation built as the aroma of baking cornbread filled the kitchen and the beans became tender on the stove.

When supper was ready, she would ladle generous servings into each bowl—seven hungry family members gathered around, each hoping for a bit of luck. Hidden among the beans, the elusive red bean waited to be discovered. The moment of revelation was always met with excitement and laughter, as the fortunate recipient discovered the prized red bean in their bowl. The reward was simple but coveted: a reprieve from that evening's kitchen duties. For a child, the surprise was nothing short of breathtaking—a small victory that made the meal so memorable.

Through my grandmother's creativity and love, ordinary moments were transformed into lasting legacies, and I am forever thankful for the stories that keep those memories alive.

The Kitchen Chair

A sturdy chair and an old crank telephone—it was all he needed to catapult him into the music arena.

Story has it that when my dad was about five years old, he would often stand proudly atop a sturdy chair, his small frame elevated just enough to command the attention of the congregation at Immanuel Lutheran Church in Petersburg, Nebraska. With a voice that carried clear and true, he sang to the group of appreciative parishioners, his mother beaming with pride from the pews. She always said he had a remarkable gift—a voice that made every hymn feel like a personal message to those listening.

But even at such a young age, my dad's ambitions stretched far beyond the church walls. Inspired by the applause and encouragement he received, he began to dream of sharing his music with a wider audience. One afternoon, driven by a child's boundless curiosity and a dash of mischief, he climbed onto the kitchen chair at home, reached for the heavy phone receiver and dialed the "general" number—a line typically reserved for emergencies and important announcements throughout Boone County.

To the surprise of the operator and anyone else who happened to be listening in on the line, my dad launched into his favorite Lutheran hymn, "Looking Beyond." His clear, earnest voice traveled through the wires, echoing across the county and delighting neighbors who recognized the lyrics. The story quickly spread: the little boy with the big voice had found a way to bring music into homes near and far, turning an ordinary day into something memorable.

What began as a simple act of childhood bravado—standing on a kitchen chair and singing into a telephone—became the foundation for a lifetime of sharing his talent through music. And to think, it all started with a kitchen chair, a hymn, and the courage to consider looking beyond.

Mama's Red Boots

*She wasn't about to give up without a fight—
it really came down to who was going
to learn a valuable lesson.*

It was a story that I never tired of hearing, told to me more than once by my mama. She always laughed heartily when reliving the fond memory—especially at the role her dad played and how he made a painful reckoning so much easier to deal with. It was a valuable lesson learned, with a very happy ending.

"Mary, stop singing in class," her second-grade teacher, Mrs. Olson, reprimanded.

"But I'm *not* singing," Mary defended, posturing for a possible confrontation. "I was humming 'do-re-me-fa-so-la-ti-do' and that's not a song, so I *can't* be singing."

"Don't argue with me, young lady," the teacher corrected, this time with a harsher tone. "You were *indeed* singing."

"No, I *wasn't*." Mary had no intention of giving up without a fight. Afterall, her dad was a well-known music director at the church, and he certainly would confirm that humming musical notes was not the same as singing a song. End of story.

Even standing in the corner of the classroom proved an ineffective deterrent for the little girl's stubborn refusal to admit the error of her ways. It would take a personal visit by Mrs. Olson to Mary's home, and clarification by her dad to settle the feud once and for all.

"Mary, you *were* singing when you hummed the musical scale," he explained, taking note of the tears beginning to well in the eyes of his young daughter. "Furthermore, because you argued with your teacher, you will apologize."

Mary lowered her head and remorsefully expressed her regret for arguing. Further, her dad insisted that she apologize to her entire class the next day for causing such a scene. Mary was horrified to think of what awaited her the following day and rushed to her bedroom in tears.

The next morning, before Mary left for school, her dad handed her a big white box. To her surprise, the box showcased a brand-new pair of red boots! She was thrilled and wasted no time slipping on the boots and skipping off to school to take care of second-grade business.

The Old Opera House

*The town revival drew a much bigger
crowd than expected—
and then, right in the middle of a rousing sermon,
the old floor began to sag.*

Several years ago, when my dad's memory was still vibrant, a conversation at the dining room table yielded a sweet story about life in Tilden, Nebraska in the early 1930s. He recalled, "My grandmother, Ingeborg, was a stickler for church attendance and insisted that the entire family be present for services." He shook his head and then smiled. "My grandfather, Olav, on the other hand was often sick with a headache and excused himself from church unless it was Christmas." Dad shifted in his chair and rested his arm on the table while traveling the archives of memory. "I remember there was to be a revival on the upper floor of the old opera house on Main Street. Of course, Grandma made the trip to the farm to inform us that we would all be attending the week-long services, no excuses."

Tilden businessman, Martin Juelson owned the opera house, and Dad recalled that on the ground level of the building he ran a small grocery store. Martin always looked forward to community plays, musicals, and revival meetings that were frequently held on the second story because it was profitable for his grocery business.

As an eight-year-old boy, Dad was delighted that the store shelves were always stocked with an abundance of candy bars, peanuts, and sodas in preparation for the large revival gathering. He also remembered that the meeting had drawn such a crowd, that the upper floor began to sag in the middle. Several strong men were called upon to go out and haul back whatever they could find to prop up and strengthen the floor until the event was over. Precious memories.

Night Rider

Would the brothers be able to keep their guilty secret? To do otherwise might be a death sentence.

As a boy, my dad's brother Virgil was known for his fiery temper—a "short fuse" that could ignite into a near-fatal punch if anyone dared provoke him. This notorious trait, rather than deterring his younger siblings, became a source of endless amusement and irresistible temptation. For the mischievous younger brothers, Virgil's quick temper was like a challenge, an open invitation to test the boundaries of brotherly mischief and see just how far they could push before facing his wrath.

One warm summer night in Nebraska, the three brothers decided to embark on an adventure beneath the open sky. They each prepared to sleep outdoors, choosing their own carts as makeshift beds. The air was thick with humidity, the scent of new-mown hay, and the distant chirp of crickets—the boys relished the freedom of a night spent under the stars. To ensure a peaceful slumber, each cart was carefully secured with bricks placed in front of the wheels, a precaution against any accidental midnight journeys down the hillside.

But as the moon climbed higher and the world grew quiet, the younger brothers shared a mischievous glance. They waited patiently, listening to the steady rhythm of Virgil's breathing, and the telltale sign that he had finally drifted off to sleep. With well-practiced stealth, they crept over to his cart and quietly removed the bricks that kept it in place. In the stillness of the night, they slipped back into their own carts, pretending innocence and sleep.

Moments later, gravity took over. Virgil's cart began to roll, slowly at first, then gathering speed as it sailed down the hillside. The sudden motion jolted him awake, but by the time he realized what was happening, he was already halfway down the slope, powerless to stop the wild night ride. The younger brothers lay perfectly still, barely daring to breathe, their hearts pounding with a mix of fear and exhilaration.

When Virgil finally returned, his expression registering both suspicion and fury, he carefully inspected his brothers for any sign of movement. He knew, as did they, that the slightest twitch or smirk would be enough to unleash his legendary temper. Sensing the danger, the younger boys remained motionless, their expressions blank, determined to keep their secret safe. That night, the prank went unpunished, but the memory of their daring escapade—and the thrill of outwitting Virgil—became a cherished, long-held secret between them.

Afterword

Having entered the autumn season of my life, I find myself drawn ever more often into thoughtful solitude, where golden memories swirl through my mind like the vibrant leaves of fall, each one carrying its own fragrance of sweet remembrance. In these quiet moments, I linger over the tapestry of my days, pondering each thread—some bright with laughter, others shadowed by loss, but all woven together into the story of a life well-lived. There is a profound comfort in the simple things: the gentle hush of early morning, the warmth of a familiar melody, the steady presence of loved ones. These small blessings offer a calm assurance, a gentle reminder that change is inevitable, but hope endures.

As I reflect on the passage of time, I am keenly aware of how the world has shifted around me. Now, in the conservative autumn years, I look back with longing to softer, gentler times—a world where neighbors were like family, and strangers were simply friends waiting to be discovered. It was an era when elders were honored, their wisdom sought and cherished, and children learned the invaluable art of listening, absorbing the fantastic stories passed down by those who came before. I sometimes catch myself humming "A Dream is a Wish Your Heart Makes," and in those moments, I am transported to a place where kindness was commonplace, and community was the heartbeat of daily life.

Yes, I know I am showing my age, but there is a reluctance to settle for a world that seems, in many ways, to have lost its sense of direction. Too often, the essential elements that create priceless legacies—compassion, respect, and the willingness to remember—are cast aside in favor of fleeting distractions. Yet, I remain steadfast in my belief that the true measure of a life is found in the legacies we nurture, the stories we share, and the love we leave behind. These are the treasures that endure the test of time, growing sweeter with each passing day.

Throughout my journey, I have experienced a myriad of poignant moments—love that lifted my spirit, loss that deepened my understanding, the incomparable joy of children, and a growing appreciation for the wonders of God's creation. I have traveled the world, yet kept my own circle small, finding contentment in quiet reflection and the less-traveled paths through forests of golden leaves. In this autumn season of life, I have come to realize that existence is not measured by grand achievements or material gain, but by the collection of moments—each one a gift, each one a lesson, each one a thread in the fabric of who we are.

May we all come to cherish the moments, honor the stories, and nurture the legacies that will one day become the golden memories of those who follow. For in remembrance, there is hope; in gratitude, there is peace; and in love, there is the promise that our stories will endure.

The Good Old Days
Ah, the good old days, with memories like gold,
Where traditions were born, and stories told,
Though time moves on, their essence is sure,
With every remembrance, legacies endure.
~ D. L. Norris

www.ingramcontent.com/pod-product-compliance
Lightning Source LLC
Chambersburg PA
CBHW042143160426
43201CB00022B/2385